MANAGING

PARAEDUCATORS

in YOUR

SCHOOL

How to Hire, Train, and Supervise Non-Certified Staff

Nancy K. French

CORWIN PRESS, INC.
A Sage Publications Company
Thousand Oaks, California

For information:

Corwin Press, Inc.
A Sage Publications Company
2455 Teller Road
Thousand Oaks, California 91320
www.corwinpress.com

Sage Publications Ltd.
6 Bonhill Street
London EC2A 4PU
United Kingdom

Sage Publications India Pvt. Ltd.
M-32 Market
Greater Kailash I
New Delhi 110 048 India

Printed in the United States of America

Library of Congress Cataloging-in-Publication Data

French, Nancy K.
Managing paraeducators in your school: How to hire, train, and supervise non-certified staff / by Nancy French.
        p. cm.
Includes bibliographical references and index.
ISBN 0-7619-7785-6 (cloth)
ISBN 0-7619-7786-4 (pbk.)
1. Teachers' assistants—Training of—United States—Handbooks, manuals, etc.
2. Teaching teams—United States—Handbooks, manuals, etc. I. Title.
LB2844.1.A8 F74 2002
371.14'124—dc21
        2002007008

This book is printed on acid-free paper.

02 03 04 05 06 10 9 8 7 6 5 4 3 2 1

Acquisitions Editor:	Robert D. Clouse
Corwin Editorial Assistant:	Erin Clow
Production Editor:	Diana E. Axelsen
Typesetting:	Bramble Books
Cover Designer:	Michael Dubowe
Production Artist:	Janet Foulger
Indexer:	Judy Hunt

Contents

Preface

As a young teacher, I made many mistakes in my work with para-educators. In 1971, I moved from Chicago to a rural town in Colorado. The fourth-grade team shared the time of one paraeducator who had lived in the community for many years, knew the families of the children in our school, and played bridge with the superintendent's wife. She was my mother's age (which I thought was old then) and I was 23. I was intimidated by her knowledge of the community and reluctant to give her directions. The similarity to my mother was too strong. In my family, daughters didn't tell mothers what to do—it was the other way around. I wasn't at all prepared for the role reversal that was seemingly required.

Moreover, I didn't know what she was supposed to do; there was no job description. I assumed that I should have known and that I was supposed to be in charge. I was afraid to ask about her job description, fearing that I would reveal my ignorance and lack of experience. Teaching positions weren't easy to come by in those days, and I didn't want to risk my position by appearing weak or unprepared.

In the absence of any preparation to direct the work of a paraeducator, and in the absence of support from the principal on what would be appropriate direction, I fumbled my way through that year. I was certain that the bridge club received reports of my teaching ability that were not flattering to me. In fact, I came to treat her as a spy, unwelcome in my room. I sent her out of the room to run errands or perform menial tasks as much as possible. When she didn't return the following year, I was immensely relieved. Unfortunately, the district lost a valuable resource.

Fortunately for me, I was able to work with intelligent, kind, intuitive, and effective paraeducators in the next few years and I gained a little maturity in the process. My early difficulties caused me to search out information on working with paraeducators and to learn how to improve my supervisory skills.

More than 25 years later, I conducted an interview with teachers to determine how they were handling their work with paraeducators. I asked one young teacher how she knew what to do, and she said, "There really isn't any training out there, but hopefully after a year or two things get better." At that point, I realized that teachers who were graduating in the year 2000 were getting no more preparation to work with paraeducators than those of us who become teachers in 1970. Now, I have had the opportunity to teach supervisory skills to nearly 2000 teachers and to provide them with tools to use in their work with paraeducators. In teaching, I have also learned.

This book is intended to serve district-level administrators with responsibilities for curriculum and instruction, special education, bilingual education, and ESL, as well as Title I and other remedial programs. It is also written for the school administrator who is serious about supporting good teamwork among the teachers and paraeducators in the building. Finally, this book is for teachers and all the school professionals who work directly with paraeducators.

ACKNOWLEDGMENTS

I would like to acknowledge the work of the one million paraeducators who are the unsung heroes of our educational system, working for low pay and little recognition to help students learn. The paraeducators with whom I've worked have helped me understand why they take this job in the first place and why they stay over time. I also want to pay tribute to all the teachers and administrators who have participated in the Paraeducator Supervision Academy and have learned how to create effective teacher-paraeducator teams. I appreciate all the teachers and paraeducators who have participated in my research studies over the past 10 years and acknowledge the substantial contribution they have made to this effort.

I also want to acknowledge the important contributions of Maggie Emery and Carol Long who first conceived of the idea of using worksheets as a platform for team communication and the development of personalized job descriptions.

In addition, I want to thank those who helped me get the ideas down on paper. Ritu Chopra helped me think through the first two chapters and how to present the pros and cons of employing paraeducators. Karen Friedman helped with several of the tables and read every word as a critical friend and editor, asking questions and offering suggestions. Barbara Stimson first pilot-tested the Special Education Paraprofessional Support Checklist and offered her help in designing an instrument that would be helpful to others. Ann Vidolovits-Moore put the Special Education Paraprofessional Support Checklist to use on a large scale in her district to assure me that it had broad applicability.

About the Author

 **Nancy K. French, Ph.D.,** is Associate Research Professor at the University of Colorado at Denver and the director of The PAR^{2}A Center. The PAR^{2}A Center has developed the CO-TOP Model for training paraeducators. The CO-TOP Model includes an extensive curriculum for the inservice preparation of paraeducators and trains teachers and other school professionals to supervise and provide instruction to paraeducators. In addition, the CO-TOP Model includes the Paraeducator Supervision Academy, a course that prepares inservice teachers and administrators to work more effectively with paraeducators. The PAR^{2}A Center houses research projects that examine legislation, policies, and practices regarding the employment, supervision, and training of paraeducators.

1 Employing Support Personnel in Schools

THE RATIONALE FOR PARAEDUCATORS

In a well-run school, support personnel are nearly invisible. They perform their duties behind the scenes. Yet, you probably realize that, in your school, those who provide instructional support are critical to the functioning of your school programs.

There are many job titles for instructional support personnel in schools. Sometimes they are called teacher aides, but a shift toward more respectful titles is noticeable across the country. Titles such as "playground aide" are being changed to "campus supervisor" and "teacher aide" is being changed to "educational assistant" or "instructional assistant" and frequently "paraprofessional" or "paraeducator."

Whatever title is used, persons who hold such positions may be generally classified as paraeducators—persons who hold positions that are alongside, at the side of, or beside a professional in education. The work that paraeducators do is intended to support the work of professionals. In education, like medicine, dentistry, and law, we see increasing numbers of paraeducators employed to deliver efficient, timely, and compassionate services.

Consider the story of McKinley Elementary School described in Box 1.1. McKinley isn't different from most elementary schools in urban and suburban areas where there is diversity among students. Then, think about your own school to see how it compares.

Why Employ Paraeducators in School Programs?

There are 10 good reasons to employ paraeducators to work alongside the professionals in your school.

Complex Student Population

The complexity of the student body in many schools today is much greater than it was in the 1970s and 1980s. There are three factors that contribute to this complexity. First, there are cultural and linguistic differences. With the

1

BOX 1.1

MCKINLEY ELEMENTARY SCHOOL

At McKinley Elementary School, 21 people work in instructional support positions alongside a professional faculty of classroom teachers and art, music, and physical education teachers, as well as special education and early childhood teachers. Some paraeducators work alongside itinerant related services personnel (school psychologist, school nurse, speech-language therapist, physical therapist, occupational therapist, and an adapted physical education teacher) to provide support for McKinley students. Paraeducators also work in the school library, in the lunchroom, in the school bus loading zone, and on the playground.

- **Barbara and Mark** are paraeducators assigned to the special education program.
- **Judy** is a special education paraeducator, dedicated to a single student who needs substantial support throughout the day.
- **Estella and Diane** are schoolwide Title I program paraeducators.
- **Michelle, Kristy, Becky, Peg, Jorge, and Maria** all work as classroom paraeducators—each is assigned to a team of teachers at a particular grade level.
- **Cruz, Silvia, Amparo, and Elena** are ESL-bilingual paraeducators. They all speak both Spanish and English. Each is assigned to a particular classroom to work with monolingual Spanish-speaking students.
- **Rae and Tami** are speech-language pathology assistants (SLPAs) who deliver speech-language services to special education students under the direction of an itinerant speech-language pathologist.
- **Helen** is the health clerk and runs the school health room, distributing medications, providing routine respiratory care, and tending to minor injuries and illnesses.
- **Joye** works full time as a library assistant to manage the school's media center and assist students and teachers to support instruction and learning.
- **Lorraine and Delores** work in the lunchroom, supervising students as they eat lunch and are on the playground, and supervising students according to the recess schedule. Lorraine works in a kindergarten classroom before and after lunch and Delores works as a clerk assisting the school secretary when she is not in the lunchroom or on the playground.

influx of immigrants from Eastern Europe, Mexico, Asia, and Africa, as well as Central and South America, urban, suburban, and even rural schools now serve many students who enter school speaking languages other than English.

While schools in some urban areas have always had immensely diverse populations of students, now the rest of the country is experiencing the same situation. In central Kansas there has been a large immigration of people from Latin America to work in the meat packing industry. Rhode Island boasts a large influx of people from Cape Verde. California, Colorado, and the entire southwest section of the United States are experiencing immigration from Mexico, Central America, and South America.

Second, special education legislation and litigation opened the schoolhouse doors to children with disabilities in unprecedented numbers. Now K-12 schools include children with a range of mild, moderate, and significant disabilities. The special education process is, by definition, an individualizing process because students who require special education services have many unique needs. At the same time, there is increased awareness that all children, no matter their differences, deserve access to general education curriculum, experiences, and extracurricular activities. Recent legal decisions have supported the requests of parents of students with disabilities that the schools provide increased access to the general education curriculum. Therefore, many children with disabilities are being educated in regular classrooms where they require additional support to ensure their success in accessing the general education curriculum.

Third, socioeconomic circumstances contribute to the diversity of schools. While the economic boom of the 1990s improved the lives of many American families, there are families who did not experience the benefits of a strong economy. Children from those families come to school with fewer advantages and are at risk academically. Some schools serve a wide range of students, from those who live in multimillion dollar houses to those who live in small apartments, mobile homes, and even the backseats of cars. Poverty is a major factor in placing students at risk for educational failure. When the numbers of students living in poverty are large, the school qualifies for Title I funds. Title I funds are often used to pay salaries of paraeducators who live in the same community and share the same cultural and linguistic heritage and socioeconomic circumstances as the families served by the school.

Need for Instructional Support

The side effect of the current emphasis on high academic standards for all children and the focus on testing to determine achievement of standards is that there is now an increased need for individualized, personalized, humane, and caring instructional support for students. The increased need for human contact is central to the shift toward increased instructional roles for paraeducators and is consistent across programs. When the student population was less complex, and when there were fewer academic demands to be met, paraeducators assumed mainly clerical responsibilities. In recent years, the paraeducator role has shifted to include significantly greater responsibility for instruction. These instructional roles vary somewhat, depending on the type of program to which they are assigned, the skills and attributes they bring to the position, and the training they receive after employment.

Cost Effectiveness

While no one would claim that teachers or other school professionals are highly paid, salaries comprise the largest share of school district budgets.

Hiring nonprofessional personnel has made it possible for districts to provide services to students while balancing the budget. Paraeducators are the fastest growing segment of all school employees. And, throughout the United States, the rate of employment for paraeducators is at an all-time high. Paraeducators are typically hourly employees, paid at rates that vary according to the local economy, but tend to result in annual incomes approximately equivalent to one third of the average professional's salary. So, a paraeducator in the library and media center is likely to earn about one third of the pay of a professional school librarian who is at the midpoint on the pay scale. It makes good economic sense to employ a variety of staff members at varying pay levels if the roles can be ethically and legally differentiated, and the responsibilities distributed.

Instructional Effectiveness

The effectiveness of paraeducators who have specific training in the delivery of instruction to students with disabilities was well documented in the 1970s and 1980s. The effectiveness of paraeducators who have specific training in the delivery of services and instruction to young children has also been well documented. In 23 comparative studies, the presence of carefully trained and monitored nonprofessional teaching assistants resulted in twice as much student learning when compared with conventional teaching. In every study, some important teaching function was delegated to someone other than the teacher. Moreover, research has substantiated a positive relationship between the level of paraeducator training and student achievement outcomes. For example, studies have shown that well-trained paraeducators increased the promotion rates, standardized test scores, and attendance rates of students. One-to-one tutoring programs delivered by well-trained paraeducators were effective in accelerating student reading achievement. A combination of social skills training and paraeducator support in general education classrooms improved the behavior of students with ADHD (attention deficit hyperactivity disorder) and minimized classroom disruptions. A study of high-performing schools found that paraeducators played an important role that included both academic and managerial responsibilities. The highest-performing schools clearly delineated the roles and responsibilities of professionals and paraeducators. All staff received training to carry out specific instructional programs, and teachers and paraeducators formed effective teams. Like earlier research, this study revealed that paraeducators in high-performing schools had relevant, practical training to carry out the instructional program.

Community Connections

The use of paraeducators is widespread in schools that serve students whose primary language is other than English. In some places, paraeducators who speak the same language as students work alongside monolingual English-speaking teachers to provide academic instruction. When directed and guided to do so, paraeducators can contribute significantly to the academic achievement of students who have limited English proficiency but who are taking academic courses in English. Bilingual paraeducators in high-performing schools tend to serve as translators for families and students who speak limited

English because it is their second language. They also provide some important connections for people who live in the neighborhoods served by the school.

Sometimes, paraeducators serve as Title I community liaisons, performing a wide range of tasks ultimately designed to make life easier for kids in the classroom such as visiting the children's homes to discuss school attendance, illness, or how families can support student learning. Title I paraeducators have helped families to obtain community services and resources. In communities where poverty affects the lives of students, paraeducators may provide community linkages that are vital for the academic achievement of students.

Paraeducators are often the primary linkage between the parents of students with significant disabilities and the school. Parents rely on daily communications with paraeducators for information about the behavior and activities of their nonverbal children with disabilities. Parents report that they know and relate to paraeducators as neighbors, babysitters, and friends. Parents have said that paraeducators know their children better than the teachers and are their primary source of information about their child's school day.

Individualized Support for Including Students With Disabilities

The trend toward inclusive education of children with disabilities is growing. Increasingly, parents request inclusion for their children. Many parents of students with disabilities believe that paraeducators are critically important to the delivery of instruction and related services to students when they are included in general education classrooms. In many cases, the parents of students with disabilities request that a dedicated paraeducator be hired to assist and accompany their child throughout the school day. Parents assert that constant support for the physical, health, social, and academic needs of their children is vital to the health and safety of their children in school. General educators also believe that paraeducators are necessary if they are to have special education students in their classrooms. Teachers who are effective in including students with disabilities use paraeducator time to support the curricular and instructional adaptations they design.

Legislation and the Employment of Paraeducators

Most states have permissive language that empowers local educational agencies to hire both professional and nonprofessional personnel to carry out all the programs and services of the school. At the national level, Titles I and VII of the Improving America's Schools Act (IASA) both contain permissive language regarding paraeducators, but also place limits on the employment of paraeducators to achieve an appropriate balance of professionals and paraeducators. In the 2002 reauthorization of IASA, Title I specifies the duties that are permitted, as well as the requirements for paraeducator training and skills. The Individuals with Disabilities Education Act (IDEA) Amendments of 1997 specify that paraeducators who are adequately trained and supervised may *assist* in the delivery of special education and related services as long as they have the necessary skills and knowledge (Individuals with Disabilities Education Act of 1997, 20 U.S.C. § 1401). Moreover, IDEA indicates that paraeducator services *must* be provided to students with disabilities (including one-to-one services) if such services are necessary for a student to receive a free appropriate public education (FAPE). Recent legal decisions have addressed the "necessity of paraeducator services" (Katsiyannis, Hodge, & Lanford, 2000) by indicating that the individualized education plan (IEP) team holds the responsibility to make the determination whether a paraeducator is necessary for a FAPE.

Related Services Support for Students

Under IDEA, schools must provide "related services" as required to help students with disabilities to benefit from special education. Those related services may include health care services, therapies, or psychological services according to the individual needs of students.

Health Care Services. Health care services are one example of related services. The test for whether a service qualifies as a medical service or as a school health service is whether, legally speaking, a doctor must perform the procedure. If a nurse or other qualified person can perform the procedure, it qualifies as a required service under IDEA (IDEA Regulations, 34 C.F.R. § 300.16). The key words are "other qualified person." Courts have held that a health aide can perform such technical procedures as clean intermittent catheterization and tracheotomy tube suctioning as well as those procedures that require lesser amounts of training (e.g., dispensing oral medication) under the supervision of a school nurse. Supervision generally means that the nurse has trained the paraprofessional to perform the procedure, physically observed the paraprofessional performing the procedure correctly on the individual student, and periodically conducted follow-up observations.

Nationwide, school nurses are increasing in number, but there is an increased use of paraprofessionals in health roles as well. Technically, a school nurse holds the ultimate responsibility for all health care services and procedures and for the welfare and safety of students. The nurse may be permitted to delegate the task to a person that he or she has personally trained to perform a selected nursing task in a selected situation. Delegation also requires that the nurse continue to supervise the performance of that procedure on a regular basis. Supervision is defined as "provision of guidance by a qualified nurse for the accomplishment of a nursing task or activity with initial direction of the task or activity and periodic inspection of the actual act of accomplishing the task or activity" (Phillips & Krajicek, 1994). For students who are not covered by special education law, the requirements are a little different and often less stringent. Of course, the responsibility to protect the safety and welfare of students remains, but there is increased flexibility in how that is done. Generally, schools use health care assistants or health aides to provide routine screening, administration of minor first aid, management of routine and screening records, and dispensation of oral medications—all under the guidance of a school nurse. School nurses practice under the nurse practice act of the state and delegate tasks to others as specified in the delegatory clause of that act.

In some districts across the country, each school has a school nurse assigned and no health care assistants are used. In most districts, however, schools share nurses and in some situations nurses are stretched fairly thin across three, four, five, or more school buildings. Where nurses are shared among buildings, health care assistants who are present throughout the day are the norm. This is because there are problems associated with the hiring of fully qualified school nurses for every school building. First, cost prohibits most districts from hiring a nurse for every school. Second, availability is a factor in deciding how many fully qualified school nurses the district employs. Fully prepared school nurses are not readily available in all communities, particularly in rural areas. Often rural schools contract for nursing services through community or county agencies.

Speech and Language Therapy. Another example of related services is speech-language therapy. The employment of paraeducators in this field is less widely accepted than in nursing. However, the advantages to employing para-educators include an increased ability to serve larger numbers of students and an increased number of services to each student at a lower cost. Other reasons to employ speech-language paraeducators in education settings include the greater involvement of parents as partners in education and the inclusion of special education students throughout more classrooms and buildings than in the past. Some states have developed specific guidelines for the education, supervision, and employment of speech-language pathology assistants or para-educators. Acceptable duties for speech-language paraeducators include

- Conducting hearing screenings
- Assisting with diagnostics and progress-monitoring tests
- Checking and maintaining equipment
- Participating in research projects, inservice training, and public relations
- Assisting with schedule development
- Assisting with classroom activities
- Following treatment plans and protocols
- Documenting student progress
- Assisting with clerical work
- Reporting to supervisor
- Scheduling activities
- Preparing charts, records, and graphs

Improved Teacher-Student Ratio

Class size affects student learning. There is little disagreement that this is so, and numerous studies and meta-analyses of research have consistently associated large class size with decreased student achievement and increased teacher stress levels. Yet, schools fail to cut class sizes because of the costs. Using only teachers to decrease class size to the point where it makes a difference would mean that districts would need to hire twice as many teachers and build twice as many schools to house them.

Paraeducators are a viable alternative. Paraeducators can help effectively reduce the ratio of students to adults, if they are employed in instructional capacities, appropriately directed, and trained to perform their responsibilities. Employing paraeducators in every classroom could increase the amount and quality of instructional time for students, as well as the ability of the teacher-paraeducator team to respond in timely, compassionate ways to student emotional and behavioral needs at considerably lower cost. Other possible advantages to employing paraeducators in general education classrooms include the presence of different strengths within the classroom, providing positive role models to students, flexibility in instructional delivery, and a safer, more consistent environment. Finally, the presence of instructional paraeducators allows the teacher to spend more time on assessment and curriculum planning.

Other related benefits of employing paraeducators to improve adult-student ratios may include improved student behavior and self-concept, positive student attitudes toward learning and school, improved teacher morale, reduced teacher stress levels, and improved school-home-community relations.

Shortages of Fully Qualified Professionals

Shortages of fully qualified teachers to work in special education, bilingual education, early childhood, and early childhood special education programs have necessitated the employment of paraeducators who work under the direction of the available professionals. There are two widely different sets of assumptions regarding the employment of paraeducators to relieve the shortage of professional personnel.

The paraeducator is a future teacher. The first set of assumptions is typically found in the literature on career ladders for paraeducators and considers the paraeducator position as a preparatory stage in the development of professionals. It looks to the future, rather than to the present role of the paraeducator and is most commonly discussed in the bilingual education literature. Many districts have designed "grow your own" programs that reward and support paraeducators who pursue teacher preparation. Many such programs are funded by the U.S. Department of Education's Office of Bilingual Education and Minority Language Affairs. Several universities have formed coalitions that pave the paraeducator-to-teacher pathway. Recent research on paraeducators who pursue teaching degrees shows that it takes a paraeducator longer than traditional students to complete the program, but that they tend to remain in teaching positions longer.

Unfortunately, teacher preparation programs reserve the courses on instructional methods and curricular delivery to students in their final stages of teacher preparation. Most teacher preparation programs require junior or senior status before applying to the education program, and many deny access to the courses that would be most beneficial to paraeducators. If teacher preparation programs would allow beginning college students to take those classes, they would be providing a service to the schools whose paraeducators need immediate training in instruction to carry out their work assignments.

Paraeducator is a legitimate job. The second set of assumptions focuses on the current role and status of the paraeducator rather than the future role. This perspective is based on research on the current role of paraeducators in special education, general education, Title I, and bilingual education. This research typically shows that most paraeducators choose not to become teachers or do not pursue teacher preparation for other reasons. There is an extensive literature base that takes this perspective and demonstrates that paraeducators make significant contributions to the education of a variety of students and emphasizes the importance of targeted training and career development for these individuals.

CHAPTER SUMMARY

There are 10 good reasons to employ paraeducators in your school. They include

1. Increasing complexity of student population

2. Increased need for instructional support

3. Cost effectiveness

4. Effectiveness of paraeducators in delivering instruction

5. Enhanced community connections

6. Individualized supports for students with disabilities

7. Legislation that permits or requires paraeducator assistance

8. Need to provide related services

9. Improved teacher-student ratios

10. Shortages of qualified professionals

The programs that typically employ the most paraeducators are special education, bilingual education, and Title I. In addition, paraeducators are employed in early childhood, general education K-12 classrooms, health rooms, and library and media centers. Paraeducators fill many educational needs, work alongside school professionals to deliver timely, compassionate services and instruction to students, and help connect the school to the community it serves.

However, within each of these programs there are controversial issues that affect hiring decisions. Chapter 2 discusses the potential problems associated with the employment of paraeducators in each of these programs.

2 Potential Problems With Paraeducators: Finding Solutions

PROBLEMS ASSOCIATED WITH SCHOOL PROGRAMS

Although the reasons for employing paraeducators are compelling, there are some potential problems. However, there are ways to avoid the repercussions associated with each problem. This chapter provides guidelines to assist administrators in making the right decisions and tables to identify the needs and a building's readiness to employ paraeducators.

One-to-One Dedicated Paraeducators in Special Education

Critics recognize that untrained paraeducators hired to serve individual students may inadvertently separate students from general education curriculum and teachers even though students are ensured such access in the law. There have been reports that paraeducators sometimes intervene inappropriately (e.g., helping too much with students' assignments, providing assistance where none is needed). There is also concern that paraeducators pose social barriers between students. Intensive artificial instructional supports from specialists and paraprofessionals cannot be replicated in postschool environments, so natural supports are preferable.

Parents continue to support the use of paraeducators because they recognize the safety and health needs of their children at school. Parents are also concerned that busy classroom teachers have too little time to provide individualized academic, communication, social, or behavioral assistance to their children and that using other students to provide supports is an inadequate response to a very real, and often intense, need.

At the same time, districts are seeking to provide the right amount and types of services in the most economical way possible. They need to ensure that the resources they use to provide services are affordable. Therefore, guidelines for the employment of one-to-one dedicated paraeducators in inclusive classes are essential. The Special Education Paraeducator Support Checklist (Table 2.1) may be used to minimize the potential problems with the employment of special education paraprofessionals who are dedicated to working with individual students one-to-one. Use of the form may accomplish three things.

First, it documents the need for paraeducator support and causes the planners to consider other alternatives, such as natural supports already available in the environment, prior to or during a special education IEP meeting. By indicating the nature of the need, the context, location, or situation in which the need is most evident, the time period(s) during which the need exists, the alternatives considered, and the amount and duration of assistance required, the IEP team can easily document those thought processes.

Second, assigning responsibility for training the paraeducator or other person who provides the needed supports will ensure that it gets done. Providing training to the paraeducator ensures that the student will receive the best possible instructional support. This also protects the school from the liability associated with providing services through untrained staff.

Third, supervisory responsibilities are specified on the form. Specifying supervisory responsibility helps to ensure that the paraeducator is, in fact, assisting appropriately. Documenting the plan for supervision also limits liability associated with providing services through unsupervised staff.

Title I Paraeducators

Some critics say that poor achievement among students receiving Title I services has resulted from the common practice of hiring paraeducators. They have recommended that paraeducators be systematically removed from Title I programs. Other critics recommend that most Title I paraeducators perform only clerical tasks.

Defenders of paraeducators admit that student achievement is not as it should be, but point out that the blame is probably misdirected. Low achievement is more likely to result from multiple, interrelated factors such as program models that fail to provide a clear delineation of the roles and responsibilities of professionals and paraeducators, training for those responsibilities, and appropriate direction and supervision by qualified teachers.

Poorly differentiated roles and responsibilities and the lack of direction exist because teachers were not prepared for their roles as supervisors. Yet, training for the teachers who direct the work of Title I paraeducators and training designed specifically for paraeducators is allowed under the current law. Indeed, federal statistics show that about 27% of Title I funds go to the professional development of teachers every year. For relatively little more, paraeducators could receive training on all the recommended topics and teachers could be trained to provide appropriate supervision to Title I paraeducators.

The Title I Self-Assessment Checklist (Table 2.2) lists recommendations for practices associated with the employment of paraeducators in Title I programs and schools. To determine whether employing paraeducators is right for your Title I targeted or schoolwide program, score your ability to address each of the best practices listed. Use of this form can help ensure that paraeducators are being used in ways that will contribute to the achievement of the students served in the program.

Table 2.1 Special Education Paraeducator Support Checklist
Student: _____ Date: _____

Student Issues and Needs Profile[a]	Place Time Level Duration[b]	Who Could Assist?[c]	Training Plan[d]	Supervision[e]
1. Safety issues ○ Wanders off/runs away ○ Hurts self ○ Falls ○ Puts inedible items in mouth ○ Hurts others ○ _____ ○ _____ ○ _____	**Place:** **Time(s):** **Level:** Low Medium High **Duration:** Permanent Temporary	○ Age-peer student ○ Older student ○ General education teacher ○ Special education teacher ○ Class/program paraprofessional ○ 1:1 designated paraprofessional ○ Parent volunteer	**Training needed/ Who delivers** ○ _____/_____ ○ _____/_____ ○ _____/_____ ○ _____/_____ ○ _____/_____ ○ _____/_____	**Check all who share supervisory responsibility and name lead person** ○ General education teacher ○ Special education teacher ○ Occupational or physical therapist ○ Speech-language therapist ○ School psychologist ○ Nurse ○ Vision or hearing specialist ○ Other professional _____ ○ Lead _____
2. Physical needs ○ Restroom/diapers ○ Orientation/mobility ○ Eating/feeding ○ Dressing ○ Breathing/respiration ○ Medication ○ Equipment (e.g., hearing aids, wheelchairs) ○ Posture, positioning ○ Medicaid-billable procedures ○ Has individualized health plan in place ○ Other _____ ○ _____	**Place:** **Time(s):** **Level:** Low Medium High **Duration:** Permanent Temporary	○ Age-peer student ○ Older student ○ General education teacher ○ Special education teacher ○ Class/program paraprofessional ○ 1:1 designated paraprofessional ○ Parent volunteer	**Training needed/ Who delivers** ○ _____/_____ ○ _____/_____ ○ _____/_____ ○ _____/_____ ○ _____/_____ ○ _____/_____	**Check all who share supervisory responsibility and name lead person** ○ General education teacher ○ Special education teacher ○ Occupational or physical therapist ○ Speech-language therapist ○ School psychologist ○ Nurse ○ Vision or hearing specialist ○ Other professional _____ ○ Lead _____

Table 2.1 continued

Student Issues and Needs Profile[a]	Place Time Level Duration[b]	Who Could Assist?[c]	Training Plan[d]	Supervision[e]
3. Communication needs ○ Instruction in use of technology (including Braille, sign language) ○ Cues/prompts to use technology ○ Programming of device(s) ○ Cues/prompts to communicate with peers/adults ○ Interpretation ○ Cues/prompts to use articulation skills ○ Voice, breathing ○ Other _____	**Place:** **Time(s):** **Level:** Low Medium High **Duration:** Permanent Temporary	○ Age-peer student ○ Older student ○ General education teacher ○ Special education teacher ○ Class/program paraprofessional ○ 1:1 designated paraprofessional ○ Parent volunteer	**Training needed/ Who delivers** ○ ___/___ ○ ___/___ ○ ___/___ ○ ___/___ ○ ___/___ ○ ___/___	**Check all who share supervisory responsibility and name lead person** ○ General education teacher ○ Special education teacher ○ Occupational or physical therapist ○ Speech-language therapist ○ School psychologist ○ Nurse ○ Vision or hearing specialist ○ Other professional _____ ○ Lead _____
4. Behavioral needs ○ Disruptive behaviors (e.g., noises, hitting) ○ Self-stimulation ○ Resists changing activity ○ Refuses to follow directions ○ Takes others' things ○ Sits passively, doesn't engage in activity ○ Makes bad choices ○ Needs specifics of Individual Behavior Plan monitored, supported ○ Other _____ ○ _____	**Place:** **Time(s):** **Level:** Low Medium High **Duration:** Permanent Temporary	○ Age-peer student ○ Older student ○ General education teacher ○ Special education teacher ○ Class/program paraprofessional ○ 1:1 designated paraprofessional ○ Parent volunteer	**Training needed/ Who delivers** ○ ___/___ ○ ___/___ ○ ___/___ ○ ___/___ ○ ___/___	**Check all who share supervisory responsibility and name lead person** ○ General education teacher ○ Special education teacher ○ Occupational or physical therapist ○ Speech-language therapist ○ School psychologist ○ Nurse ○ Vision or hearing specialist ○ Other professional _____ ○ Lead _____

Table 2.1 continued

Student Issues and Needs Profile[a]	Place Time Level Duration[b]	Who Could Assist?[c]	Training Plan[d]	Supervision[e]
5. Social needs ○ Prompts/cues to interact with peers ○ Social instruction ○ Protection from peers ○ Peer instruction on how to interact with student ○ Adult instruction on how to interact with student ○ Other _____	**Place:** **Time(s):** **Level:** Low Medium High **Duration:** Permanent Temporary	○ Age-peer student ○ Older student ○ General education teacher ○ Special education teacher ○ Class/program paraprofessional ○ 1:1 designated paraprofessional ○ Parent volunteer	**Training needed/ Who delivers** ○ ___/___ ○ ___/___ ○ ___/___ ○ ___/___ ○ ___/___ ○ ___/___	**Check all who share supervisory responsibility and name lead person** ○ General education teacher ○ Special education teacher ○ Occupational or physical therapist ○ Speech-language therapist ○ School psychologist ○ Nurse ○ Vision or hearing specialist ○ Other professional _____ ○ Lead _____
6. Academic needs ○ Cues to attend to teachers ○ Cues to begin tasks ○ Cues to remain on task ○ Physical use of instructional materials ○ Modification of instructions/directions ○ Modification of materials, tasks (including Braille) ○ Adaptive equipment ○ Community-based activities ○ Job shadow, exploration ○ Work/job skill development ○ Other _____	**Place:** **Time(s):** **Level:** Low Medium High **Duration:** Permanent Temporary	○ Age-peer student ○ Older student ○ General education teacher ○ Special education teacher ○ Class/program paraprofessional ○ 1:1 designated paraprofessional ○ Parent volunteer	**Training needed/ Who delivers** ○ ___/___ ○ ___/___ ○ ___/___ ○ ___/___ ○ ___/___	**Check all who share supervisory responsibility and name lead person** ○ General education teacher ○ Special education teacher ○ Occupational or physical therapist ○ Speech-language therapist ○ School psychologist ○ Nurse ○ Vision or hearing specialist ○ Other professional _____ ○ Lead _____

Table 2.1   continued

a. Check all boxes that apply. Specify other needs that are not listed.

b. *Place:* Describe the location where the assistance will be provided (e.g., gym, hallway, lunchroom, classroom). *Time:* Indicate times of the school day when assistance is needed by hour or period (e.g., 9:15–10:00 am or art class). *Level:* For each student, mark the level of support needed using the following descriptions. Low – support person checks on student periodically or engages with the student for short periods of time, and provides cues, prompts, instruction, related services, or supervision that permit the student to engage in or continue with tasks reasonably independently. Medium – support person spends approximately one-half of the school day providing cues, prompts, instruction, related services, or supervision that permit the student to engage in or continue with tasks for which partial participation is acceptable and independence is not the short-term objective. High – support person spends a majority of the school day with the student providing cues, prompts, instruction, related services, or supervision that permit the student to engage in or continue with tasks for which partial participation, rather than independence, is the eventual goal. *Duration:* Circle the anticipated duration of the support necessary, using the following descriptions: Permanent – the amount of support, whether low, medium, or high, is provided on a long-term, no-end-in-sight basis to assist a student to engage in or continue with tasks for which he/she is unlikely to gain independence before the next meeting. Temporary – the amount of support, whether low, medium, or high, is provided temporarily to assist a student in gaining independence in new environments, activities, acquisition of new concepts, or English as a second language. The assumption here is that the student will gain some level of independence during the designated time period and will need less support in future time periods.

c. Indicate possible persons who could provide the necessary assistance to the student, considering what other adults and student supports are already in place in each environment. Providing assistance through people who are already in the environment reduces the chance that the student will become overly reliant on adult attention, increases the likelihood that he or she will learn to rely on natural supports in the environment, and reduces the chance that the student will be inadvertently isolated from peers and general education curriculum and instruction.

d. For each student need, time, and place of assistance, and for each person who provides assistance, indicate the type of training that will be provided including the person who holds responsibility for ensuring the delivery of training.

e. Indicate the person(s) who will supervise the assisting person(s). You may specify which of the seven supervisory functions each supervisor will perform. The seven supervisory functions are orientation to the job, delegation and direction of daily tasks, planning (based on IEP objectives), scheduling, on-the-job training, performance monitoring and feedback, and managing the work environment (including conflict management, communications, problem solving).

Table 2.2 Title I Self-Assessment Checklist

Best Practice[a]	Timeframe[b]	Rating of Our Ability to Do This[c]	Who Does It?[d]
Seek applicants for Title I paraprofessional positions who meet the highest educational standard ○ 2 years of college or AA degree, or ○ Passing score on competency assessment, and ○ Skills in literacy and math instruction	⇨ Prior to employment	3 = No problem 2 = Possible 1 = Very difficult 0 = No way	**Check all who share responsibility and name lead person** ○ General education teacher ___ ○ Title I teacher ___ ○ Administrator ___ ○ Other professional ___ Lead person ___
Provide specific orientation to school/personnel ○ Orientation to layout of building ○ Introductions to personnel ○ Review staff handbook, emergency procedures ○ Confidentiality issues ○ Discipline/behavior policies	⇨ First day of employment ⇨ Before working with students	3 = No problem 2 = Possible 1 = Very difficult 0 = No way	**Check all who share responsibility and name lead person** ○ General education teacher ___ ○ Title I teacher ___ ○ Administrator ___ ○ Other professional ___ Lead person ___
Examine and compare work styles and preferences ○ Use Worksheets 1–3 ○ Conduct orientation interview	⇨ Within first week of employment	3 = No problem 2 = Possible 1 = Very difficult 0 = No way	**Check all who share responsibility and name lead person** ○ General education teacher ___ ○ Title I teacher ___ ○ Administrator ___ ○ Other professional ___ Lead person ___
Provide specific, personalized job description ○ Use Worksheets 4–6 **Plan for specific training needs and prepare paraprofessional to engage actively in development activities** ○ Use Worksheet 7	⇨ Within first week of employment	3 = No problem 2 = Possible 1 = Very difficult 0 = No way	**Check all who share responsibility and name lead person** ○ General education teacher ___ ○ Title I teacher ___ ○ Administrator ___ ○ Other professional ___ Lead person ___

Table 2.2 continued

Best Practice[a]	Timeframe[b]	Rating of Our Ability to Do This[c]	Who Does It?[d]
Provide written instructional plans for paraprofessional	⇧ Updated weekly as necessary	3 = No problem 2 = Possible 1 = Very difficult 0 = No way	**Check all who share responsibility and name lead person** ○ General education teacher ___ ○ Title I teacher ___ ○ Administrator ___ ○ Other professional ___ Lead person ___
Monitor and observe during instruction Provide feedback about performance	⇧ Once weekly	3 = No problem 2 = Possible 1 = Very difficult 0 = No way	**Check all who share responsibility and name lead person** ○ General education teacher ___ ○ Title I teacher ___ ○ Administrator ___ ○ Other professional ___ Lead person ___
Include in team meetings **Require use of appropriate interpersonal and communication skills**	⇧ Weekly	3 = No problem 2 = Possible 1 = Very difficult 0 = No way	**Check all who share responsibility and name lead person** ○ General education teacher ___ ○ Title I teacher ___ ○ Administrator ___ ○ Other professional ___ Lead person ___
Train in specific literacy, math, and learning-strategy instructional methods, in methods of managing behavior, and teaching replacement behaviors	⇧ Weekly or as available	3 = No problem 2 = Possible 1 = Very difficult 0 = No way	**Check all who share responsibility and name lead person** ○ General education teacher ___ ○ Title I teacher ___ ○ Administrator ___ ○ Other professional ___ Lead person ___

Table 2.2 continued

Best Practice[a]	Timeframe[b]	Rating of Our Ability to Do This[c]	Who Does It?[d]
Train to manage individual students and small groups of students	⬦ Weekly or as available	3 = No problem 2 = Possible 1 = Very difficult 0 = No way	**Check all who share responsibility and name lead person** ○ General education teacher ___ ○ Title I teacher ___ ○ Administrator ___ ○ Other professional ___ Lead person ___
Train in use of high- and low-tech assistive devices, including computers	⬦ Weekly or as available	3 = No problem 2 = Possible 1 = Very difficult 0 = No way	**Check all who share responsibility and name lead person** ○ General education teacher ___ ○ Title I teacher ___ ○ Administrator ___ ○ Other professional ___ Lead person ___
Total Scores[e]	⬦	/30	

a. Consider each recommended practice and how it might be carried out in your school or district.

b. Note the appropriate timeframe for completing each practice. Consider the time demands as suggested for each recommended practice. Consider the time demands that the person who carries out this practice will have to give up something else that he or she currently does to be able to fit this in.

c. Use the rating scale to indicate your ability to address the recommended practice, considering the time demands, personnel skills, and availability of training resources. 3 = *No problem*: Personnel currently have the skills to perform all tasks associated with this practice. 2 = *Possible*: Requires the establishment of new systems, plans, and responsibilities for professional personnel. May require training for professional personnel to develop skills. We can arrange to get training for professionals. 1 = *Very difficult*: It will be very difficult to establish the new systems, plans, and responsibilities for professional personnel. The training for professional personnel to develop skills will be very difficult to arrange and hold. 0 = *No way*: The demands of the practice exceed our ability to address them.

d. This column consists of lists of professional personnel who are the most likely candidates for each responsibility. Check the person most likely to be assigned or to share this responsibility in your school. In the case of shared responsibility, one person should be named as the Lead Person.

e. Add the scores for each item. *Highest possible score is 30*: You are able to meet the highest ethical and educational standards. *Ratings of 20 and above*: Your school can employ paraprofessionals and ensure that their employment will support student achievement, meet high ethical standards, and protect you from liability associated with poor practices. *Ratings of 10–19*: Your school or district is not well prepared to follow through with training and support for the professional personnel who will perform each responsibility. If you choose to employ paraprofessionals, consider that you may not be able to meet your student achievement goals and you may place yourselves in a position that is difficult to defend in terms of ethics. *Ratings of 0–10*: Your school is not a good candidate for the employment of paraprofessionals in Title I programs. This score indicates that the most ethical and educationally sound decision is to employ only fully prepared reading specialists and or reading teachers in Title I positions.

Bilingual Education and English as a Second Language (ESL) Programs

One solution often applied to the problem of teacher shortages in bilingual and ESL programs is to employ paraeducators to fill positions that remain unfilled by certified teachers. Unfortunately, this solution causes many other problems. When paraeducators take the place of a certified teacher, acceptable student achievement levels cannot be expected. There are three common mistakes that should be avoided in the employment of ESL or bilingual paraeducators.

First, it is a serious mistake to allow paraeducators to provide primary instruction to students for whom English is their second language. Often the paraeducators are completely unprepared to do so. Most paraeducators lack even basic preparation for the role of paraeducator, and they certainly have no preparation to make the curricular, instructional, assessment, and behavior management decisions that a professional teacher is expected to make. It is a serious breach of ethical standards to employ unprepared personnel to do the teacher's job. Most of all, it is a serious impediment to the academic welfare of the students.

Second, a common problem is that paraeducators provide concurrent translation of instruction. Paraeducators often do this without an understanding of the possible or likely outcomes. While students may prefer to have English language instruction translated into their native language, the practice ultimately is likely to limit their academic performance. First, translated instruction is likely to lose some of the quality of the original conceptual explanation. Second, reliance on translation of academic instruction into their native language also will limit the students' proficiency, spontaneity, and academic performance in English. Third, it allows the students to selectively attend to the paraeducator speaking the native language rather than the teacher who is speaking in English.

Third, a common mistake is to allow paraeducators to become the sole linkage between the school and the parts of the community for whom English is not the home language. While paraeducators play an important connector role, they should not be seen as the only contact or sole liaison with the community. Administrators and teachers should remain visible and actively engaged in communications with the families of their students. Trust levels may never be established between the teacher and the family if the only person to speak face-to-face with family members is the paraeducator. One way to accomplish this is to train paraeducators to provide interpretation and translation between these families and the schools.

The ESL-Bilingual Consulting Teacher Model. The solution to these problems relies on the availability of some ESL or bilingual teachers who have in-depth knowledge of language acquisition, ESL and bilingual methods, and the general education curriculum to guide and direct the work of paraeducators and of monolingual English-speaking classroom teachers, who may have no experience teaching students for whom English is not the first language. It also depends on the ability of the district to provide appropriate inservice training to para-

> **BOX 2.1**
>
> **ESL-BILINGUAL CONSULTING TEACHER MODEL IN ACTION**
>
> Mr. Field's social studies class is studying world population. Mr. Field lectures, in English (his only language), about population shifts and immigration. Then, Ms. Ramirez, a paraeducator assigned to his classroom, follows through by holding an additional conversation with students in their native language about the world population concepts that Mr. Field taught. The discussion includes exploration and enhancement of the concepts that Mr. Field used and asks about the students' experiences with immigration, discusses what they've read in their textbook, and asks students to reflect on related concepts. The conversation, held in the students' native language, enriches their understanding of world population. The ESL teacher, Ms. Arroyo, previously provided training and direction to Ms. Ramirez so she knew not to translate Mr. Field's instruction.

educators. Paraeducators in ESL and bilingual programs need to understand the fundamental purposes of various ESL or bilingual program models and to know the basics of second language acquisition and bilingual and ESL instructional methods, as well as the basics of instruction that are needed by paraeducators in all other aspects of education. Box 2.1 provides an example of the ELS-Bilingual Consulting Teacher Model.

The ESL-Bilingual Consulting Teacher Model Checklist (Table 2.3) will help you determine whether your circumstances support the use of a consulting bilingual-ESL teacher model to employ paraeducators in ways that avoid common problems and that support sound educational practice. It also provides the opportunity to reflect on some ideas about what would be required to change to a consulting teacher model. Complete the checklist while making the decisions on how to staff your bilingual or ESL program.

School Library and Media Center

A functional school library and media center is unlikely to occur by accident. Thoughtful planning for student needs and teacher needs is essential. Yet, critics point out that many school libraries and media centers have an untrained paraeducator at the circulation desk and lack adequate planning and guidance. If appropriate training and supervision cannot be provided, it is probably not wise to employ paraeducators in school libraries and media centers.

Professional school librarians and media center specialists are prepared to create collections of age-appropriate materials that support the reference needs of students and that provide supplemental readings relevant to the curriculum. They usually hold teacher certification as well as library science degrees so they have both curricular knowledge and knowledge of how to support that curriculum through the selection of appropriate materials. Library science and media programs also prepare school librarians and media specialists to catalog

Table 2.3 The ESL–Bilingual Education Consulting Teacher Model Checklist

Do we have sufficient numbers of ESL–bilingual education teachers and specialists to:	Yes or No	If no, what else could we do to create improved circumstances?
a) Supervise the work of paraprofessionals?		○ Increase our recruiting efforts?
b) Assess students' English proficiency and academic progress?		○ Provide training regarding supervision of paraprofessionals to the ESL–bilingual teachers currently employed?
c) Plan English or native language instruction that paraprofessionals can carry out?		○ Change the caseload of certified ESL–bilingual teachers to encourage a consultative model rather than a direct teaching model?
d) Consult with classroom teachers to plan academic instruction that accommodates the needs of English language learners?		○ Provide training on consultation and collaborative skills to current ESL–bilingual teachers?
e) Provide some of the direct instruction to students?		○ Provide training on assessment-driven planning to upgrade the skills of the current ESL–bilingual teachers?
		○ Other _____

Can we redefine the role of the ESL–bilingual teacher as the supervisor of paraprofessionals to:	Yes or No	If no, what can we do to create improved circumstances?
f) Orient paraeducators to the language policy, ESL–bilingual program design, and level or focus of language instruction?		○ Provide district-developed orientation packets or materials to teachers?
g) Provide lesson, unit, and lesson-adaptation plans for paraeducators?		○ Provide training on how to plan for curricular and instructional adaptations for the English language learner?
h) Provide schedules for paraeducators?		○ Provide training on developing schedules for multiple people, so students receive language development and curricular supports as necessary?
i) Direct the work of paraeducators?		○ Provide training on how to direct the work of paraprofessionals?
j) Provide on-the-job training to paraeducators?		○ Provide training on how to observe, monitor, and document the work of paraeducators?
k) Monitor and observe paraeducators while working with students?		○ Provide training on how to provide training, feedback, and coaching to paraeducators?
l) Provide feedback and coaching to paraeducators?		○ Provide training on conducting effective meetings with paraeducators and colleagues for the purposes of communication, problem solving, and conflict management?
m) Provide data to administrator for annual evaluation?		
n) Meet with paraeducators to resolve problems and manage conflicts?		○ Provide training on the use of translators?
o) Communicate with families, using translation as necessary?		○ Other _____

Table 2.3 continued

Can we hire sufficient numbers of paraeducators:	Yes or No	If no, what can we do to create supportive circumstances?
Who speak, read, and write in both their native language and in English?		○ Provide English language instruction to paraeducators whose proficiency in English is not at an academic level?
Who can translate and interpret between their native language and English?		○ Provide training in translation and interpretation skills to paraeducators with appropriate language skills?
		○ Other _____
Can we avoid placing the full responsibility on paraeducators for teaching ESL by redefining the roles and responsibilities to:	**Yes or No**	**If no, what can we do to create supportive circumstances?**
p) Supplement and assist teachers rather than replace them?		○ Rework paraeducator job descriptions?
q) Collect student achievement data to provide to teacher or specialist who assesses students?		○ Provide training to paraeducators specifically designed for them and their redefined roles and responsibilities rather than training designed for teachers?
r) Follow lesson, unit, and adaptations plans?		○ Provide training that specifies
s) Provide services to students according to schedule?		○ how to follow lesson plans and how to carry out various types of instructional sequences?
t) Follow the directions of ESL-bilingual education teacher regarding ESL-bilingual education practices and the direction of the classroom teacher regarding the academic curriculum?		○ how to use effective communication skills and participate as a team member in problem solving and conflict management?
u) Meet with teachers to receive training and coaching to perform instructional tasks effectively?		○ how to participate actively in performance appraisal and staff development activities?
v) Participate actively in their own performance appraisals?		○ Assess paraeducators' skills in both oral and written language?
w) Speak, read, and write in both languages?		○ Other _____

materials to maximize their potential use by students and faculty. Cataloging requires substantial judgment, even when cataloging services are used. It is especially important to have a fully certified librarian at the secondary level, even though the librarian may be assisted by one or more paraeducators. Elementary school libraries may operate day to day with a paraeducator at the desk, but appropriate direction, training, and supervision by a qualified school library and media specialist is necessary. The School Library and Media Assistant Supervision Checklist (Table 2.4) can be used to ensure that library assistants are appropriately supervised and directed by a professional school librarian, whether the librarian is on site or located centrally in the district.

General and Special Education Classrooms at K-12 and Early Childhood Levels

There are numerous problematic circumstances in early childhood, elementary, and secondary classrooms and in early childhood and K-12 special education classrooms in which the employment of paraeducators has been less than satisfactory. The following problems have been shown to be problematic:

- Paraeducators perform only clerical work

- Paraeducators are hired with no minimum qualifications or prior training

- Paraeducators are not given appropriate on-the-job training

- Paraeducators are not provided direction or guidance by the teacher

- Teachers feel threatened by the presence of the paraeducator

These problems are related to unsatisfactory student outcomes. Considering each of the identified problems individually may help to avoid them.

Clerical Role. At one time, some believed that if teacher aides were to take attendance, grade practice papers, collect lunch money, handle fund-raiser materials, or take charge of other noninstructional activities such as setting up for activities or cleaning up after events, teachers would have more time to teach students. However, recent observations in classrooms where paraeducators held clerical roles showed that teachers were not spending any more time in either reading or math instruction than teachers in classes without paraeducators. If increased instructional time is desired, then teachers and paraeducators should be scheduled to provide instruction simultaneously and minimize time lost to menial tasks through efficient management techniques.

Lack of Specified Job Qualifications. In some places, paraeducators have been hired with little attention to qualifications, and their presence has failed to improve student achievement. Minimal job qualifications should include a high school diploma or its equivalent, high school equivalent literacy skills, sufficient interpersonal communication skills for effective team participation, and mature workplace conflict management. Personal qualities such as love for children, flexibility, empathy, and sense of humor have been mentioned as

Table 2.4 School Library-Media Assistant Supervision Checklist

Best Practice	Timeframe	Rating	Who Does It?
Seek trained applicants for library assistant position	⇧ Prior to employment	3 = No problem 2 = Possible 1 = Very difficult 0 = No way	**Check all who share responsibility and name lead person** ○ School-based professional librarian ___ ○ District-level professional librarian ___ ○ Administrator ___ ○ Other professional ___ Lead person ___
Provide specific orientation to the school and personnel ○ Orientation to layout of building ○ Introductions to personnel ○ Review staff handbook and emergency procedures ○ Confidentiality issues ○ Discipline and behavior policies	⇧ First day of employment ⇧ Before working with students	3 = No problem 2 = Possible 1 = Very difficult 0 = No way	**Check all who share responsibility and name lead person** ○ School-based professional librarian ___ ○ District-level professional librarian ___ ○ Administrator ___ ○ Other professional ___ Lead person ___
Examine and compare work styles and preferences ○ Use Worksheets 1–3 ○ Conduct orientation interview	⇧ Within first week of employment	3 = No problem 2 = Possible 1 = Very difficult 0 = No way	**Check all who share responsibility and name lead person** ○ School-based professional librarian ___ ○ District-level professional librarian ___ ○ Administrator ___ ○ Other professional ___ Lead person ___

Table 2.4 continued

Best Practice	Timeframe	Rating	Who Does It?
Provide specific, personalized job description ○ Use Worksheets 4-6 **Plan for specific training needs and prepare paraprofessional to engage actively in development activities** ○ Use Worksheet 7	⇧ Within first week of employment	3 = No problem 2 = Possible 1 = Very difficult 0 = No way	**Check all who share responsibility / Lead person** ○ School-based professional librarian ___ ○ District-level professional librarian ___ ○ Administrator ___ ○ Other professional ___ Lead person ___
Provide written library procedures for paraeducator to implement	⇧ Updated weekly as necessary	3 = No problem 2 = Possible 1 = Very difficult 0 = No way	**Check all who share responsibility / Lead person** ○ School-based professional librarian ___ ○ District-level professional librarian ___ ○ Administrator ___ ○ Other professional ___ Lead Person ___
Monitor and observe performance of library-media center management tasks	⇧ Once weekly	3 = No problem 2 = Possible 1 = Very difficult 0 = No way	**Check all who share responsibility and name lead person** ○ School-based professional librarian ___ ○ District-level professional librarian ___ ○ Administrator ___ ○ Other professional ___ Lead person ___
Provide feedback about performance	⇧ Quarterly	3 = No problem 2 = Possible 1 = Very difficult 0 = No way	**Check all who share responsibility and name lead person** ○ School-based professional librarian ___ ○ District-level professional librarian ___ ○ Administrator ___ ○ Other professional ___ Lead person ___

Table 2.4 continued

Best Practice	Timeframe	Rating	Who Does It?
Include in team meetings Require use of appropriate interpersonal and communication skills	⬆ Weekly	3 = No problem 2 = Possible 1 = Very difficult 0 = No way	**Check all who share responsibility and name lead person** ○ School-based professional librarian _____ ○ District-level professional librarian _____ ○ Administrator _____ ○ Other professional _____ Lead person _____
Train in specific library procedures, use and monitoring of computer and Internet-based student research, in methods of managing behavior, etc.	⬆ Weekly or as available	3 = No problem 2 = Possible 1 = Very difficult 0 = No way	**Check all who share responsibility and name lead person** ○ School-based professional librarian _____ ○ District-level professional librarian _____ ○ Administrator _____ ○ Other professional _____ Lead person _____
Total Scores	⬆	/30	

desirable qualities for paraeducators. Work habits such as reliability, promptness, initiative, and ability to take direction have also been mentioned.

Lack of Prior Preparation. Often, there is no attempt to locate applicants who have prior preparation. While it is true that there are only a few preparation programs to provide trained K-12 classroom paraeducator applicants, it is also true that some programs do exist and more would emerge if there were increased demand for trained personnel. Chapter 4, "Recruiting and Hiring Paraprofessionals," includes a table of some of the programs that prepare paraeducators. Fortunately for early childhood classrooms, there has been a Child Development Associate (CDA) credentialing program at the national level since 1971. There are many CDA programs at the community or junior college level that prepare people to provide developmentally appropriate instruction and care to young children.

Lack of Orientation to the Position. Many paraeducators begin working with students immediately, without prior orientation to the school, personnel, district discipline and safety policies or procedures, or program schedules or routines. The potential liability is enormous when this is the case. If a paraeducator has had no orientation, any unexpected event at school could result in improper action by the paraeducator and may jeopardize the safety and welfare of students. A formal orientation should be conducted for every new employee.

Lack of Ongoing and Inservice Training. Over the years, a lack of appropriate paraeducator training has been a pervasive problem. Reid and Johnston (1978) warned, "Using non-skilled assistants, however well meaning they may be, is not sound if we are to meet our obligation to provide educational and developmental programming. . . . The answer, then, is the provision of paraeducator personnel who have been trained in the methodology of learning and management" (p. 84). Yet, systematic training for paraeducators remains the exception rather than the rule.

Isolation of Low-Achieving Students From Teacher. Sometimes teachers assign paraeducators to work with the lower-performing students, believing that this practice would give the teacher more time to work with higher-achieving students. This practice is problematic because it denies low-achieving students the benefit of the best help available—the teacher. However, although some teachers believed that they had spent more instructional time with higher-achieving students, that belief was not substantiated by observational data.

Threat to Teacher. Some teachers reported that they felt threatened having another adult in the room. They thought that the paraeducator might judge them and then talk about them to others, indicating a lack of a trusting team relationship. Some were also concerned about losing the affection of their students. Teachers have reported ambiguous feelings about paraeducator assistance in the classroom. While they want the help, classrooms have long been the domain of the teacher. The loss of autonomy is met with reluctance in some situations.

Lack of Preparation to Supervise. Teachers have no preparation to supervise paraeducators or to understand the differences in the respective roles of paraeducators and teachers. As a result, some teachers have used paraeducators inappropriately—either assigning tasks that should have been maintained by the teacher or failing to assign tasks that could have improved the teacher's productivity and effectiveness.

The Classroom Paraeducator Checklist (Table 2.5) provides a way to consider the appropriateness of assigning paraeducators to classrooms based on the ability of the school to capitalize on the positive features of paraeducator employment and minimize the problems.

Health Care Services

There remain numerous concerns associated with the employment of health assistants. The concerns come from both the nursing professionals and the health care paraeducators themselves. Both are concerned that inappropriate care provided to a student because of the lack of adequate paraeducator training or appropriate supervision could result in serious harm to the student and legal liability for both the district and the school nurse. The school nurse, of course, risks her license. The district is liable financially and ethically.

The American Federation of Teachers (AFT) has included a chapter in *The Medically Fragile Child in the School Setting* that provides guidelines on the appropriate employment, training, and supervision of nonmedical personnel in schools (AFT, 1997). The following three precautions will protect the safety and welfare of students, paraeducators, and nurses.

1. Require appropriate training for all school personnel working with students who have health needs.

2. Educate all school personnel regarding the legal limitations placed on them by the state's nurse practice act.

3. Provide job descriptions that clearly define the roles and responsibilities of all school personnel regarding the health needs of students.

The School Health Assistant Best Practices Checklist (Table 2.6) can be used to assess your situation. It includes recommended best practices and allows reflection on the ability of a building or district to achieve the best practice. The scoring mechanism will help make the decision about whether hiring health assistants is a safe practice for your building or district.

Speech and Language Pathology

There are two major issues regarding use of speech-language pathology paraeducators. First, concerns about the lack of training for speech-language pathology paraeducators are significant. Studies have shown that some school districts have provided continuing education and on-the-job training to speech-language paraeducators, but haven't done a good job of documenting the training. Districts also tend to provide brief amounts of training on a variety of topics because of limited resources. There is concern that brief overviews may provide too little information to affect practice. The minimum standard for

(text continued on p. 36)

Table 2.5 Classroom Paraeducator Checklist

Best Practice[a]	Timeframe[b]	Rating[c]	Who Does It?[d]
Seek applicants for classroom paraprofessional positions who meet the highest educational standard	⇧ Prior to employment	3 = No problem 2 = Possible 1 = Very difficult 0 = No way	**Check all who share responsibility and name lead person** ○ General education teacher(s) ___ ○ Grade level/subject team ___ ○ Administrator ___ Lead person ___
Consider the comfort level of the classroom teacher(s) with having other adults in the classroom	⇧ Prior to employment or during first few weeks of employment	3 = No problem 2 = Possible 1 = Very difficult 0 = No way	**Check all who share responsibility and name lead person** ○ General education teacher(s) ___ ○ Grade level/subject team ___ ○ Administrator ___ Lead person ___
Ensure that teachers have clear understanding of appropriate role differentiation and preparation to supervise	⇧ Prior to employment or during first few weeks of employment	3 = No problem 2 = Possible 1 = Very difficult 0 = No way	**Check all who share responsibility and name lead person** ○ General education teacher(s) ___ ○ Grade level/subject team ___ ○ Administrator ___ Lead person ___
Provide specific orientation to the school and personnel ○ Orientation to layout of building ○ Introductions to personnel ○ Review staff handbook and emergency procedures ○ Confidentiality issues ○ Discipline and behavior policies	⇧ First day of employment ⇧ Before working with students	3 = No problem 2 = Possible 1 = Very difficult 0 = No way	**Check all who share responsibility and name lead person** ○ General education teacher(s) ___ ○ Grade level/subject team ___ ○ Administrator ___ Lead person ___

Table 2.5   continued

Best Practice[a]	Timeframe[b]	Rating[c]	Who Does It?[d]
Examine and compare work styles and preferences ○ Use Worksheets 1–3 ○ Conduct orientation interview	⇧ Within first week of employment	3 = No problem 2 = Possible 1 = Very difficult 0 = No way	**Check all who share responsibility and name lead person** ○ General education teacher(s) ____ ○ Grade level/subject team ____ ○ Administrator ____ Lead person ____
Provide specific, personalized job description ○ Use Worksheets 4–6 **Plan for specific training needs and prepare paraprofessional to engage actively in development activities** ○ Use Worksheet 7	⇧ Within first week of employment	3 = No problem 2 = Possible 1 = Very difficult 0 = No way	**Check all who share responsibility and name lead person** ○ General education teacher(s) ____ ○ Grade level/subject team ____ ○ Administrator ____ Lead person ____
Provide written plans for paraprofessional to implement	⇧ Updated weekly as necessary	3 = No problem 2 = Possible 1 = Very difficult 0 = No way	**Check all who share responsibility and name lead person** ○ General education teacher(s) ____ ○ Grade level/subject team ____ ○ Administrator ____ Lead person ____
Monitor and observe during instruction and provide feedback about task performance	⇧ Once weekly	3 = No problem 2 = Possible 1 = Very difficult 0 = No way	**Check all who share responsibility and name lead person** ○ General education teacher(s) ____ ○ Grade level/subject team ____ ○ Administrator ____ Lead person ____
Include in team meetings **Require use of appropriate interpersonal and communication skills**	⇧ Quarterly	3 = No problem 2 = Possible 1 = Very difficult 0 = No way	**Check all who share responsibility and name lead person** ○ General education teacher(s) ____ ○ Grade level/subject team ____ ○ Administrator ____ Lead person ____

Table 2.5   continued

Best Practice[a]	Timeframe[b]	Rating[c]	Who Does It?[d]
Provide job-specific training to paraeducators on ○ Management of large and small groups ○ Use of high- and low-tech devices, including computers ○ Specific literacy, math, and learning-strategy instructional methods ○ Methods of managing behavior ○ Methods for teaching replacement behaviors	⬠ Weekly or as available	3 = No problem 2 = Possible 1 = Very difficult 0 = No way	**Check all who share responsibility and name lead person** ○ General education teacher(s) ____ ○ Grade level/subject team ____ ○ Administrator ____ Lead person ____
Total Scores[e]		/30	

a. Consider each recommended practice and how it might be carried out in your school or district.

b. Consider the time demands as suggested for each recommended practice. In many cases, the person who carries out this practice will have to give up something else, to be able to fit this in.

c. Use the rating scale to indicate your ability to address the recommended practice, considering the time demands, personnel skills, and availability of training resources. 3 = No problem: Personnel currently have the skills to perform all tasks associated with this practice. 2 = Possible: Requires the establishment of new systems, plans, and responsibilities for professional personnel. May require training for professional personnel to develop skills. We can arrange to get training for professionals. 1 = Very difficult: It will be very difficult to establish the new systems, plans, and responsibilities for professional personnel. The training for professional personnel to develop skills will be very difficult to arrange and hold. 0 = No way: The demands of the practice exceed our ability to address them.

d. Consists of lists of professional personnel who are the most likely candidates for each responsibility. Check the person most likely to be assigned or to share this responsibility in your school. In the case of shared responsibility, one person should be named as the lead person.

e. Add the scores for each item. Highest possible score is 30: You are able to meet the highest ethical and educational standards. Ratings of 26 and above: Your school can employ paraprofessionals and ensure that their employment will support student achievement, meet high ethical standards, and protect you from liability associated with poor practices. Ratings of 15–25: Your school or district is not well prepared to ensure sound educational and ethical practices around the use of paraprofessionals. If you choose to employ paraprofessionals, consider that you may need to organize for further training or supervision, or you may not meet your student achievement goals and you may place yourselves in a position that is difficult to defend ethically. Ratings of 0–14: Your school is not a good candidate for the employment of classroom paraprofessionals.

Table 2.6   School Health Assistant Best Practices Checklist

Best Practice[a]	Timeframe[b]	Rating[c]	Who Does It?[d]
Seek trained applicants for health assistant position	⇧ Prior to employment	3 = No problem 2 = Possible 1 = Very difficult 0 = No way	**Check all who share responsibility and name lead person** ○ School-based licensed nurse ___ ○ District-level licensed nurse ___ ○ Administrator ___ ○ Other professional ___ Lead person ___
Provide specific orientation to the school ○ Orientation to layout of building ○ Introductions to personnel ○ Review staff handbook and emergency procedures ○ Confidentiality issues ○ Discipline and behavior policies ○ Layout of the health room ○ Procedures for administering medications ○ Location of health records	⇧ First day of employment ⇧ Before working with students	3 = No problem 2 = Possible 1 = Very difficult 0 = No way	**Check all who share responsibility and name lead person** ○ School-based licensed nurse ___ ○ District-level licensed nurse ___ ○ Administrator ___ ○ Other professional ___ Lead person ___
Examine and compare work styles and preferences ○ Use Worksheets 1–3 ○ Conduct orientation interview	⇧ Within first week of employment	3 = No problem 2 = Possible 1 = Very difficult 0 = No way	**Check all who share responsibility and name lead person** ○ School-based licensed nurse ___ ○ District-level licensed nurse ___ ○ Administrator ___ ○ Other professional ___ Lead person ___
Provide specific, personalized job description ○ Use Worksheets 4–6 **Plan for specific training needs and prepare health assistant to engage actively in development activities** ○ Use Worksheet 7	⇧ Within first week of employment	3 = No problem 2 = Possible 1 = Very difficult 0 = No way	**Check all who share responsibility and name lead person** ○ School-based licensed nurse ___ ○ District-level licensed nurse ___ ○ Administrator ___ ○ Other professional ___ Lead person ___

Table 2.6 continued

Best Practice[a]	Timeframe[b]	Rating[c]	Who Does It?[d]
Provide written health care and health screening procedures for health assistants ○ Ensure access to applicable state publications ○ Ensure access to district policies and procedures ○ Ensure access to building-level policies, safety practices, and procedures	⇧ Updated weekly as necessary	3 = No problem 2 = Possible 1 = Very difficult 0 = No way	**Check all who share responsibility and name lead person** ○ School-based licensed nurse ___ ○ District-level licensed nurse ___ ○ Administrator ___ ○ Other professional ___ Lead person ___
Train in specific health room procedures ○ Health room management tasks ○ Health services to students (e.g., tracheotomy tube suction, nebulizer treatment, catheterization) ○ Handling of emergencies ○ Use of universal precautions ○ Administration of medications ○ Safe storage of equipment and materials ○ Other ___	⇧ Once weekly	3 = No problem 2 = Possible 1 = Very difficult 0 = No way	**Check all who share responsibility and name lead person** ○ School-based licensed nurse ___ ○ District-level licensed nurse ___ ○ Administrator ___ ○ Other professional ___ Lead person ___
Monitor and observe performance of ○ Health room management tasks ○ Health services to students (e.g., tracheotomy tube suction, nebulizer treatment, catheterization) ○ Handling of emergencies ○ Use of universal precautions ○ Administration of medications ○ Safe storage of equipment and materials ○ Other ___	⇧ Quarterly	3 = No problem 2 = Possible 1 = Very difficult 0 = No way	**Check all who share responsibility and name lead person** ○ School-based licensed I nurse ___ ○ District-level licensed nurse ___ ○ Administrator ___ ○ Other professional ___ Lead person ___

Table 2.6 continued

Best Practice[a]	Timeframe[b]	Rating[c]	Who Does It?[d]
Provide feedback about performance	⇧ Weekly	3 = No problem 2 = Possible 1 = Very difficult 0 = No way	**Check all who share responsibility and name lead person** ○ School-based licensed nurse ___ ○ District-level licensed nurse ___ ○ Administrator ___ ○ Other professional ___ Lead person ___
Include in team meetings **Require use of appropriate interpersonal and communication skills**	⇧ Weekly or as available	3 = No problem 2 = Possible 1 = Very difficult 0 = No way	**Check all who share responsibility and name lead person** ○ School-based licensed nurse ___ ○ District-level licensed nurse ___ ○ Administrator ___ ○ Other professional ___ Lead person ___
Total Scores[e]		⇧ /30	

a. Consider each recommended practice and how it might be carried out in your school or district.

b. Note the appropriate timeframe for completing each practice. Consider the time demands as suggested for each recommended practice.

c. Use the rating scale to indicate your ability to address the recommended practice, considering the time demands, personnel skills, and availability of training resources. *3 = No problem:* Personnel currently have the skills to perform all tasks associated with this practice. *2 = Possible:* Requires the establishment of new systems, plans, and responsibilities for professional personnel. May require training for professional personnel to develop skills. We can arrange to get training for professionals. *1 = Very difficult:* It will be very difficult to establish the new systems, plans, and responsibilities for professional personnel. The training for professional personnel to develop skills will be very difficult to arrange and hold. *0 = No way:* The demands of the practice exceed our ability to address them.

d. Consists of lists of professional personnel who hold the responsibility. In the case of shared responsibility, one person should be named as the lead person.

e. Add the scores for each item. *Highest possible score is 30:* You are able to meet the highest ethical and legal standards. *Ratings of 20 and above:* Your school can employ health assistants and ensure that their employment will support student safety and protect you from liability associated with poor practices. It is essential to follow through on training and supervision. *Ratings of 10–19:* Your school or district is not well prepared to ensure ethical and legal practices around the use of health assistants. If you choose to employ health assistants, consider that you may be putting students at some risk and you may place yourselves in a position that is difficult to defend legally. *Ratings of 0–10:* Your school is not a good candidate for the employment of health assistants. This score indicates that the most ethical and educationally sound decision is to employ only licensed nurses for providing health-related services to students.

hiring an appropriately prepared person to work in a speech-language paraeducator position is a two-year degree or equivalent with specialized training in language development and speech therapy techniques. Many would agree that the gold standard in prior preparation for a speech-language paraeducator is a bachelor's degree in communication disorders. The gold standard is difficult to achieve in most districts.

Second, the supervision of speech-language paraeducators remains problematic. Speech-language pathologists (SLPs) are concerned about their own job security and are often uncertain about role differentiation. As a group SLPs lack preparation to supervise paraeducators because thorough preparation for paraeducator supervision is generally not included in SLP preparation programs. Many SLPs express concern about the liability associated with delegating to another person. In many ways the delegation issues are similar to those in nursing. SLPs have also voiced concerns about the increased workload associated with providing supervision and worry that delegation to a lesser-trained person compromises the quality of services to students and the possible misrepresentation of service provider qualifications.

It is obvious that when an SLP spends more time supervising paraeducators, the amount of time they spend in direct service decreases. Thus, an SLP that supervises paraeducators must have schedule adjustments that reflect the shift in duties. Assessment and monitoring the paraeducator's performance of assigned tasks must be an ongoing, integral element of the SLP position. At a minimum, supervision of speech-language paraeducators should include constant monitoring of the first 10 hours of direct student contact following training and observation on at least 10% of all sessions after the first 10 hours of observation. Thus one in every 10 sessions would be attended by the SLP, who would then observe the paraeducator and provide feedback to the paraeducator regarding task performance.

Employing paraeducators is an appropriate option for some schools and early intervention agencies when supporting state education standards and qualifications and local policies, procedures, and administrative supports exist. While a district has little control over state education standards and qualifications, policies, procedures, and supports are within the scope of responsibility of district and building-level administrators. The Speech-Language Pathology Paraeducator Employment Self-Assessment Checklist (Table 2.7) may be used to help determine whether your school or district can ethically employ paraeducators to work alongside SLP professionals.

Finally, ethical practice not only involves the detailing of what professional SLPs should do about supervision, but also includes a list of should-nots for paraeducators. To avoid misuse, the speech-language paraeducator should not

- Assess students using either standardized or informal instruments

- Interpret test results beyond prescriptions in test manuals

- Convey information to parents in the absence of or without the direction of the SLP

- Develop or modify individualized speech-language plans

Table 2.7 Speech-Language Pathology Paraeducator Employment Self-Assessment Checklist

Recommended Practice[a]	Timeframe[b]	Rating[c]	Who Does It?[d]
Seek appropriately trained applicants for SLP assistant position	⇨ Prior to employment	3 = No problem 2 = Possible 1 = Very difficult 0 = No way	**Check all who share responsibility and name lead person** ○ School-based SLP _____ ○ District-level SLP _____ ○ Administrator _____ ○ Other professional _____ Lead person _____
Provide specific orientation to the school ○ Orientation to layout of building ○ Introductions to personnel ○ Review staff handbook and emergency procedures ○ Confidentiality issues ○ Discipline and behavior policies ○ Location of student records	⇨ First day of employment ⇨ Before working with students	3 = No problem 2 = Possible 1 = Very difficult 0 = No way	**Check all who share responsibility and name lead person** ○ School-based SLP _____ ○ District-level SLP _____ ○ Administrator _____ ○ Other professional _____ Lead person _____
Examine and compare work styles and preferences ○ Use Worksheets 1–3 ○ Conduct orientation interview	⇨ Within first week of employment	3 = No problem 2 = Possible 1 = Very difficult 0 = No way	**Check all who share responsibility and name lead person** ○ School-based SLP _____ ○ District-level SLP _____ ○ Administrator _____ ○ Other professional _____ Lead person _____

Table 2.7   continued

Recommended Practice[a]	Timeframe[b]	Rating[c]	Who Does It?[d]
Provide specific, personalized job description that delineates what paraeducators may and may not do and what remains ethically the SLP's duties ○ Use Worksheets 4–6 **Plan for specific training needs and prepare SLP paraeducator to engage actively in development activities** ○ Use Worksheet 7	⇧ Within first week of employment	3 = No problem 2 = Possible 1 = Very difficult 0 = No way	**Check all who share responsibility and name lead person** ○ School-based SLP ___ ○ District-level SLP ___ ○ Administrator ___ ○ Other professional ___ Lead person ___
Provide written plans for SLP paraeducators that include ○ Individualized activities for students based on IEPs ○ Intended outcomes for students ○ Place for paraeducator to provide feedback to SLP regarding student progress (e.g., informal treatment notes)	⇧ Updated weekly as necessary	3 = No problem 2 = Possible 1 = Very difficult 0 = No way	**Check all who share responsibility and name lead person** ○ School-based SLP ___ ○ District-level SLP ___ ○ Administrator ___ ○ Other professional ___ Lead person ___
Train in specific speech and language development procedures ○ Paperwork management tasks ○ Techniques in speech therapy ○ Language development strategies ○ Appropriate use of equipment and materials	⇧ Substantial training on all topics prior to working with individual students ⇧ Ongoing training to improve practice over time	3 = No problem 2 = Possible 1 = Very difficult 0 = No way	**Check all who share responsibility and name lead person** ○ School-based SLP ___ ○ District-level SLP ___ ○ Administrator ___ ○ Other professional ___ Lead person ___
Monitor and observe performance of the paraeducator ○ Paperwork management tasks ○ Techniques in speech therapy ○ Language development strategies ○ Appropriate use of equipment and materials	⇧ First 10 hours of paraeducator practice ⇧ 10% of all practice thereafter	3 = No problem 2 = Possible 1 = Very difficult 0 = No way	**Check all who share responsibility and name lead person** ○ School-based SLP ___ ○ District-level SLP ___ ○ Administrator ___ ○ Other professional ___ Lead person ___

Table 2.7 continued

Recommended Practice[a]	Timeframe[b]	Rating[c]	Who Does It?[d]
Provide feedback about performance	⇨ First 10 hours of paraeducator practice ⇨ 10% of all practice thereafter	3 = No problem 2 = Possible 1 = Very difficult 0 = No way	**Check all who share responsibility and name lead person** ○ School-based SLP _____ ○ District-level SLP _____ ○ Administrator _____ ○ Other professional _____ Lead person _____
Include in team meetings and require use of appropriate skills ○ Interpersonal ○ Problem solving ○ Conflict management ○ Communication	⇨ Weekly or as available	3 = No problem 2 = Possible 1 = Very difficult 0 = No way	**Check all who share responsibility and name lead person** ○ School-based SLP _____ ○ District-level SLP _____ ○ Administrator _____ ○ Other professional _____ Lead person _____
Total Scores[e]	⇨		/30

a. Consider each recommended practice and how it might be carried out in your school or district.

b. Note the appropriate timeframe for completing each practice. Consider the time demands as suggested for each recommended practice.

c. Use the rating scale to indicate your ability to address the recommended practice, considering the time demands, personnel skills, and availability of training resources. 3 = *No problem:* Personnel currently have the skills to perform all tasks associated with this practice. 2 = *Possible:* Requires the establishment of new systems, plans, and responsibilities for professional personnel. May require training for professional personnel to develop skills. We can arrange to get training for professionals. 1 = *Very difficult:* It will be very difficult to establish the new systems, plans, and responsibilities for professional personnel. The training for professional personnel to develop skills will be very difficult to arrange and hold. 0 = *No way:* The demands of the practice exceed our ability to address them.

d. Consists of lists of professional personnel who hold the responsibility. In the case of shared responsibility, one person should be named as the lead person.

e. Add the scores for each item. *Highest possible score is 30.* You are able to meet the highest ethical and legal standards. *Ratings of 20 and above:* Your school can employ speech-language paraeducators and ensure that their employment will positively affect student outcomes and protect you from liability associated with poor practices. It is essential to follow through on training and supervision. *Ratings of 10–19:* Your school or district is not well prepared to ensure ethical and legal practices around the use of speech-language paraeducators. If you choose to employ them, you may be putting students at some risk for decreased success, and you may place yourselves in a position that is difficult to defend legally. *Ratings of 0–10:* Your school is not a good candidate for the employment of speech-language paraeducators. This score would indicate that the most ethical and educationally sound decision is to employ only speech-language pathologists to provide speech- or language-related services to students.

- Sign formal documents (except informal treatment notes, which are cosigned with SLP)

- Identify students for services or discharge students from service

- Disclose confidential information to persons without the right to know

- Make referrals for additional services

- Represent himself or herself as a speech-language pathologist

CHAPTER SUMMARY

The potential problems with employing paraeducators in special education, bilingual education, Title I programs, general education classrooms, library and media centers, health rooms, and speech-language programs are significant. However, these potential problems can be effectively addressed and surmounted. This chapter includes seven tables to help administrators determine whether the problems can be overcome in each situation. Each table identifies best practices and timeframes, and provides a place to indicate the person(s) who share responsibility for the practice and names the person who takes the lead. The special education table can be used to conduct a conversation about the need for employing a personal assistant or a one-to-one paraeducator for a particular student.

3 The Shifting Roles of School Professionals

CLASSROOM TEACHERS

The presence of paraeducators who provide instructional support to students *changes the role of the classroom teacher.* Some teachers welcome the changes. They recognize that students who need special education services or students with limited English language proficiency wouldn't thrive in general education classes without additional assistance. Early childhood and early childhood special education teachers also recognize that a full caseload or classroom of students with a wide range of unique needs means that they, working alone, cannot possibly provide an appropriate amount of personal attention and care for each child. These teachers regard the work that paraeducators do as necessary to their success and to the safety, health, and academic success of their students.

Today's teachers also know that the assistance they receive from paraeducators has its price. It means that they lose some of the personalized one-to-one contact with students. Sometimes, this loss of contact also means sacrificing some control. One teacher talked about the paraeducator in her classroom: "Sometimes she does more individual instruction with the kids than I do. She is the teacher when I'm not there" (French, 1998).

CONSULTING AND COLLABORATING TEACHERS AND RELATED SERVICE PROVIDERS

In consulting and collaborating teacher and service provider models in special education, Title I, and ESL-bilingual programs, the role of the professional is already vastly different from the role of the traditional classroom teacher.

Figure 3.1 is a model that illustrates the decrease in control that teachers and service providers may experience as they move away from an educational model that emphasizes individualism and individual teachers in classrooms. The shift toward the right side of the horizontal axis represents the increases

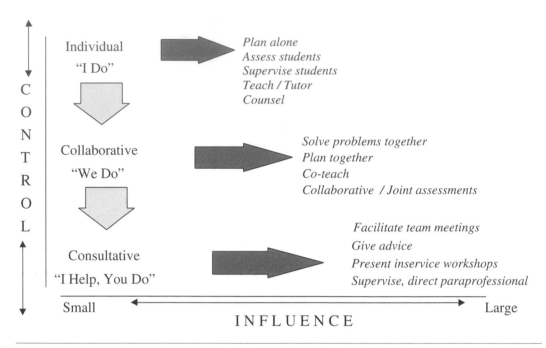

Figure 3.1. Continuum of Approaches for School Professionals

of potential influence a teacher has on students' education through collaborative and consultative work. Supervising and directing the work of paraeducators represents a maximum increase of influence on large numbers of students' educational experiences, but a loss of control over the specific daily events. The role of teachers and other service providers in schools becomes more like that of a middle-level executive, an engineer, or a doctor or lawyer, who consults with colleagues, diagnoses and plans, and then directs the work of paraprofessionals in order to meet the needs of the client or patient. In this case, the professionals plan curriculum, instruction, and appropriate adaptations and direct the paraeducator in helping to carry out the plans.

PROFESSIONAL STATUS AND SUPERVISION

In many ways, this change of roles signifies a shift to a more professional status for teachers. There has been much discussion over the years about whether teaching is a profession and how teacher qualities compare to the qualities of other professionals. Most agree that a profession is formed when members of an occupation have a knowledge base (as in engineering and medicine) and use that knowledge base to guide practice. There is also much agreement that, in professions, being prepared is essential to being a responsible practitioner and that unprepared people should not be permitted to practice. There is agreement that professional status is given to an occupation when there is a high degree of uncertainty in everyday practice that requires judgment. "Judgment," says Shulman, "is the hallmark of what it is to be a professional" (1998).

Professional judgment is required for all teachers' functions that cannot be delegated to others and for which the teacher assumes final and full responsi-

---

BOX 3.1

**SEVEN EXECUTIVE FUNCTIONS
OF PARAEDUCATOR SUPERVISION**

1. Orienting paraeducators to the program, school, and students

2. Planning for paraeducators

3. Scheduling for paraeducators

4. Delegating tasks to paraeducators

5. On-the-job training and coaching of paraeducators

6. Monitoring and feedback regarding paraeducator task performance

7. Managing the workplace (communications, problem solving, conflict management)

---

bility, even when some of the tasks that lead to completion of the professional responsibilities are assigned to others.

Berliner (1983a, 1983b) first conceived the notion of teacher as executive. He pointed out that schools are workplaces and that, whether in teaching or business, the person who runs the workplace must perform a number of executive functions. Teachers must ensure completion of and remain accountable for their five primary responsibilities. The first four are (1) planning curriculum and instruction for students, (2) assessing students both for program eligibility and for ongoing progress monitoring, (3) teaching or causing instruction to happen, and (4) collaborating with other professionals and families. The fifth responsibility, supervising paraeducators, is characterized by seven additional functions, listed in Box 3.1.

The teaching responsibilities and supervisory functions of classroom teachers vary somewhat from those of the consulting teacher or itinerant service provider. Table 3.1 lists, side by side, the variations on the responsibilities of teachers (including the supervisory functions) for two types of school professional positions—the classroom-based teacher and the consulting or itinerant professional.

TEAMWORK AMONG PROFESSIONALS WHO SHARE SUPERVISORY RESPONSIBILITIES

In combination, Figure 3.1 and Table 3.1 suggest that collaborative teamwork among professionals is essential to effective curriculum and instruction for students whose needs vary and that teamwork in carrying out the seven supervisory functions is also necessary.

In teams with a designated leader, that person is most likely to perform most of the executive functions of paraeducator supervision. However, many school

Table 3.1 Side-by-Side Variations of Classroom and Consulting Professional Roles

Consulting Teachers' and Specialists' Teaching Responsibilities and Supervisory Functions	Classroom Teachers' Teaching Responsibilities and Supervisory Functions
Planning ▷ Plan objectives that address IEP goals, language acquisition goals, behavior goals, literacy goals, health goals, etc. ▷ Prescribe types of adaptations necessary for the student to meet his or her IEP goals, language development goals, behavior goals, literacy goals, health goals, etc. ▷ Direct paraeducator to complete materials adaptations that support plans	**Planning** ▷ Plan classroom lessons and units in accordance with district curriculum standards ▷ Determine how specific adaptations that support individual learning needs should be incorporated into lesson or unit ▷ Assign paraeducator to complete materials adaptations that support the plans
Assessment ▷ Assess and evaluate individual students for program eligibility ▷ Assess and evaluate the progress of individual students	**Assessment** ▷ Assess and evaluate overall academic progress of classes of students ▷ Provide classroom data about individual students to consulting teacher or specialist
Instruction ▷ Ensure the delivery of the student's IEP, language goals, literacy goals, behavior goals, or health goals ▷ Ensure access to general education curriculum and standards	**Instruction** ▷ Ensure the delivery of the curriculum and standards appropriate to the grade level, course, or subject area ▷ Ensure that appropriate adaptations are made for students who have individualized plans
Collaboration ▷ Ensure that every classroom teacher has at least a thumbnail sketch of the individualized plans for each student on caseload ▷ Discuss the appropriate adaptations for each individual student with classroom teacher	**Collaboration** ▷ Obtain information from appropriate consulting teacher or specialist about students for whom any individualized plan exists ▷ Discuss appropriate adaptations for individual with consulting teacher or specialist

Table 3.1 continued

Consulting Teachers' and Specialists' Teaching Responsibilities and Supervisory Functions	Classroom Teachers' Teaching Responsibilities and Supervisory Functions
Orientation ▷ Orient the paraeducator to the school building, the staff, the individual students with whom he or she will work, individualized goals and needs of particular students, and the program purposes ▷ Lead the analysis of work styles and preferences for all teachers with whom paraeducator works ▷ Create personalized job description based on program and classroom needs and skills of the paraeducator in collaboration with all classroom teachers with whom the paraeducator works	**Orientation** ▷ Orient the paraeducator to the rules, routines, and procedures of the classroom, provide space in classroom for the paraeducator, and introduce paraeducator to students and other relevant adults ▷ Participate in work style and preference analysis, program needs and paraeducator skills analysis, and creation of personalized job description
Scheduling ▷ Set daily, weekly, and monthly schedules for paraeducators based on student goals, classroom lessons, and needs	**Scheduling** ▷ Communicate to consulting teacher any classroom, lesson, and unit needs that should influence the schedule
Delegation ▷ Delegate and assign tasks and duties to paraeducator regarding delivery of services according to IEP, language, behavior, literacy, and health goals	**Delegation** ▷ Delegate and assign tasks and duties to paraeducator that will enhance the content and flow of the lesson or unit in the classroom
Monitor Task Performance ▷ Monitor tasks assigned to paraeducator based on individualized goals to ensure they are performed correctly by the paraeducator ▷ Provide timely and appropriate feedback to paraeducator regarding task performance	**Monitor Task Performance** ▷ Monitor assigned tasks and duties assigned to paraeducator that are based on individualized goals and on classroom lesson and unit plans ▷ Provide timely and appropriate feedback to paraeducator regarding task performance
On-the-Job Training ▷ Train and coach in the skills required to perform assigned tasks	**On-the-Job Training** ▷ Train and coach paraeducators in the skills required to perform assigned tasks

Table 3.1 continued

Consulting Teachers' and Specialists' Teaching Responsibilities and Supervisory Functions	Classroom Teachers' Teaching Responsibilities and Supervisory Functions
Manage the Work Environment ⇨ Serve as team leader of all those involved in the individualizing aspect of the child's education: Manage intrateam communication, instructional or logistical problems, and interpersonal conflicts in the workplace that may otherwise interfere with delivery of student program	**Manage the Work Environment** ⇨ Serve as team member, contribute knowledge of curriculum and classroom instruction, participate in effective communications, and share in problem-resolution techniques and conflict management.

teams are leaderless in the sense that they do their fundamental work without a designated leader and they share the functions of team leadership. Several professional team members may share the paraeducator supervision functions. The lines of authority and communication that are so readily apparent in one-on-one supervisor-supervisee relationships become less obvious when teams share supervisory responsibilities. When this is the case, teams must clarify who will perform the executive functions of paraeducator supervision. Below are three examples of professional teams who share responsibility for the executive functions of paraeducator supervision.

Example 1: General Education Teams

An instructional team may consist of grade-level teachers or subject area teachers who share supervision of a single paraeducator. Initially, they provide orientation to the paraeducator at a team meeting, develop a personalized job description for the paraeducator, and clarify areas where they will provide on-the-job training. The team teachers plan together, determine the paraeducator's schedule, delegate tasks, and monitor the work of the paraeducator. They periodically meet with the paraeducator to communicate team and student needs, explain how to perform tasks, resolve problems and conflicts, and provide performance feedback.

Example 2: Special Education— General Education Teams in Inclusion Programs

A special education team includes various professionals—a school psychologist, physical therapist, occupational therapist, speech-language pathologist, school nurse, and special education teacher—all of whom share assessment and planning responsibilities for students with significant needs even though those students receive most of their education in a general education classroom. The critical feature here is that all the team members except the special education and general education teachers are itinerant. That is, many team members are present in the building only once or twice a week. Thus, the day-to-day scheduling, direction, and monitoring of the paraeducator's work is shared by the general education teacher and the special education teacher (who are present). Even though the two teachers assume the daily functions of supervision, the itinerant professionals provide plans, direction, on-the-job training, and monitoring of the paraeducator's task performance.

Example 3: Paraeducator Supports Students

A third example is where the paraeducator's assignment is dedicated to the support of individual students with disabilities, or groups of ESL students, who spend most of their time in general education classes. In this case, the classroom teacher assumes responsibility for planning instruction for the whole class while the special education professional or ESL teacher assumes responsibility for consulting with the general education teacher, planning the types of adaptations necessary, providing any specialized curriculum or instruction necessary, providing specific on-the-job training to the paraeducator, and monitoring student outcomes.

Each circumstance demands a unique response to the distribution of supervisory functions. Teams may use the following questions to help decide how to assign and share the seven supervisory functions.

Who Plans the Curriculum and Instruction (Including Adaptations)?

This person (or persons) may or may not be physically present. However, this person has the greatest responsibility and is accountable for outcomes. He or she holds legitimate authority for the individualized health plan, behavior plan, or language acquisition plan. This person may have been designated as the case manager or may have signed the individualized plan. This person must, at the very least, provide plans for the specific outcomes for which he or she holds responsibility. This person also provides on-the-job training and monitors the paraeducator's task performance.

Who Directs the Paraeducator on a Daily Basis?

This is the person who is physically present with the paraeducator. In cases where no single professional is physically present at all times, teams may want to identify the professionals who have proximity at various times during the paraeducator's scheduled day. This professional should, at the least, be involved in giving task direction, monitoring task performance, and providing task performance feedback to the paraeducator.

Who Provides Training for Assigned Duties?

This person may or may not be physically present on a daily basis, but must provide the training because of their licensing requirements or specific training or skill. Examples include school nurses who delegate the task of giving medications or providing other health-related services to a student. By law, the nurse must provide training and monitoring of the task. Also included here are occupational, physical, and speech-language therapists who determine the necessary interventions, but who are not physically present to carry out those interventions on a daily basis.

Who Observes and Documents Task Performance?

This may be the person who is present daily or it may be another professional team member who creates opportunities to conduct first-hand observations. In the cases of professional therapists and nurses, regulations guiding their professions require a regularly scheduled observation and documentation of paraeducator task performance.

PRINCIPALS AND DISTRICT ADMINISTRATORS

If teachers' roles shift, then so must the expectations and views of principals and district-level administrators. A building administrator must begin thinking of himself or herself as a manager of managers, or chief executive. More important, administrators both at the district and at the building levels must adjust the kinds of supports they provide to teachers—particularly to those teachers who are new to their role of supervisor.

Even though teachers are no longer solely responsible for the delivery of instruction, they remain wholly accountable for the outcomes of the instructional process. When paraeducators assist in instruction, teachers and other service providers must orient the paraeducators, plan for them, schedule their day, delegate tasks, monitor their work, train and coach them to perform their duties, and manage the work environment to ensure the quality of students' programs as well as their own professional integrity.

When this shift in teachers' roles is not welcomed, principals must help teachers recognize their rightful professional roles. Teachers who have more education as well as specific preparation to supervise paraeducators report that they are more comfortable and self-assured in the role of supervisor. Receiving "permission" to change roles combined with preparation for supervision responsibilities seems to change teachers' minds. Knowing this, administrators can make three major contributions. First, administrators can arrange for teachers and related service providers to get some training on paraeducator supervision. Second, administrators can treat teachers and other service providers as the professionals they are by respecting their decision-making skills, the right to organize their own professional lives, and their sense of responsibility for the outcomes of their work. Third, administrators can lend a sympathetic ear and offer friendly advice on how to supervise adults.

Finally, it is important to remember that even when teachers haven't had appropriate training and aren't comfortable with the roles associated with supervision, student needs rather than teacher preferences must drive staffing decisions. Thus, teachers and other professionals are sometimes compelled to collaborate with one another and to provide supervision to paraeducators because of the needs of the students in their programs. The role of administrators is to first require that this is done and to provide all the supports they possibly can to empower teachers to do their jobs well.

The Time Factor

A lack of time is a major problem in the work lives of teachers and all school professionals. At every opportunity, teachers report that the demands of large classes and caseloads, combined with schedules that permit little planning time during the school day, are a source of great stress for them. Unfortunately, the solution to this problem is apparent but not affordable. The financial means of schools do not currently support smaller classes and caseloads, more teachers, more planning hours, or fewer class responsibilities. So, teachers must make adjustments in their use of time to maximize their effectiveness without burning out. The fact is, it takes time to supervise and direct the work of paraeducators. Yet, paraeducators can perform many tasks during the school day to support students while freeing teachers' time to think, plan, assess students, collaborate with one another, and direct, monitor, and coach the paraeducator.

A word of warning is warranted. We cannot expect that teachers and other service providers will continue to do all the same things and still add more to the list. Those who try find themselves working under undue stress and they start thinking about leaving education. Working harder is not a feasible solution for most professionals. Working *smarter* is. Teachers must give up some tasks in order to perform others.

Helping School Professionals Work Smarter

Delineation of Roles and Responsibilities

Administrators can support teachers and service providers by helping them delineate the roles and responsibilities of professionals and paraeducators. To do so, it helps to know the legal, liability, and ethical issues associated with the assignment of tasks to paraeducators. Thus, administrators may want to discuss three sets of considerations with teachers and service providers who must decide what tasks to assign to paraeducators.

Legislation. Teachers and administrators must know and consider the state laws governing who teaches and pertinent policies of their state board of education as well as any local district policies or procedures. Although the 1997 Amendments to the Individuals with Disabilities Education Act (IDEA) specify that "Paraprofessionals who are adequately trained and supervised may assist in the delivery of special education and related services" (Part B, Section 612 (a) (15)), states may impose different restrictions or standards. The state's statutory authority for employing teachers and paraeducators often provides the final word on what teachers and paraeducators may or may not do. For example, Colorado Revised Statutes (CRS) specify that school districts may employ paraprofessionals to "assist certificated personnel in the provision of services related to instruction or supervision of children . . ." (CRS 22-32-110

(I) (ee)). The Iowa Administrative Code (IAC) authorizes the employment of paraprofessionals, other special education assistants, educational aides, and Title I instructional aides and requires paraeducators to complete an inservice training program during the first year of employment. Administrators may want to provide information about the laws and rules of their state that pertain to the employment of paraeducators to teachers and other service providers.

Liability. Risks to students and to personnel comprise the second set of considerations. Risks that may be tolerated are often defined by liability guidelines that vary by district and are usually recommended to the local school board or school committee by the school district's attorney or risk manager. Generally, there are three levels of responsibility for limiting the risks for students and personnel that are consistent across districts and states. Those responsibilities may be delineated as shown in Table 3.2.

Ethics. Ethically, teachers cannot assign instructional tasks to a person who has no preparation to perform them. In practice, this means that administrators and teachers must seriously consider the competencies and skills of each paraeducator before assigning a task. It also implies that teachers and administrators share the responsibility to train and coach the paraeducator to perform certain tasks when those tasks are essential to the student or the program. Or, when they can't provide the training, it means that they share the responsibility of finding the appropriate training for the paraeducator.

Administrators and teachers together must consider the formal or informal training the paraeducator has to perform every assigned task. Few paraeducators have preservice preparation. The paraeducator may have little preparation to teach, manage behavior, or understand the developmental needs, communication needs, or health concerns of students.

Even with training, there are a few responsibilities that, ethically speaking, should never be assigned to paraeducators. Certain tasks remain the sole responsibility of the person with the professional license or certificate with the caveat that some professional responsibilities are shared with the families of students with disabilities. While paraeducators assigned to special education programs may contribute information to IEP decisions, goals, and objectives, decisions are made by teams of professionals in partnership with families.

Box 3.2 lists task categories that, ethically speaking, may be delegated to paraeducators if the paraeducator is trained and if the tasks are planned, directed, and monitored by the school professionals who maintain responsibility for them.

Scheduling and Improving Time Use

Administrators should help teachers to manage the functions of supervision. One important aspect to consider is *when* the supervisory responsibilities are performed. Teachers report that they spend time outside the student-contact day to plan the schedule, design or prescribe appropriate learning activities for the paraeducator to use with students, and meet with the paraeducator for

Table 3.2 Responsibilities for Liability

Administrator Responsibilities	Professional Service Delivery Team Member Responsibilities	Paraeducator Responsibilities
⇨ Develop and disseminate written safety procedures and policies for all types of instructional programming	⇨ Provide access to all written and nonwritten procedures and policies that guide student safety and welfare	⇨ Fully understand and apply written safety procedures of the administrative unit
⇨ Provide district-level and building-level orientation to new and returning paraeducators	⇨ Orient the paraeducator to classroom and program rules, routines, procedures, and practices	⇨ Carry out and support all classroom and program rules, routines, procedures, and practices
⇨ Provide appropriate ongoing, systematic inservice training to all those (including paraeducators) who carry out the instructional program	⇨ Decide or prescribe appropriate risks as well as limitations for groups of students and individual	⇨ Exercise prudent judgment relative to the safety and welfare of students
⇨ Provide an environment in which effective communication and teamwork among team members may occur	⇨ Provide written plans for instruction and curricular adaptations to the paraeducator	⇨ Implement the written instructional, curricular, and adaptations plan as directed
⇨ Provide mentoring and guidance to professionals who supervise paraeducators	⇨ Establish and maintain a record-keeping system where paraeducators contribute data about student behavior and progress	⇨ Take data and keep appropriate records and documentation relative to student performance and behavior and contribute to the record-keeping system
	⇨ Communicate all decisions, plans, policies, and prescriptions to paraeducators	⇨ Communicate all relevant observations, insights, or information about students to professional team members
	⇨ Review with the paraeducator all the needs or circumstances of students that may affect their safety or welfare	⇨ Be aware of and heed the physical, behavioral, emotional, and educational needs of students that may affect their safety and welfare

---

BOX 3.2

LEGITIMATE PARAEDUCATOR TASK CATEGORIES

1. Data Collection and Reporting

2. Activity Preparation and Follow-up

3. Team Participation and Membership

4. Clerical Work

5. Ethical Practice

6. Supervision of Groups of Students

7. Delivery of Instruction

8. Health and Personal Related Services

9. Other Tasks as Assigned

---

on-the-job training, coaching, and feedback. In return for the investment of time outside of the students' school day, the presence of a paraeducator doubles the amount of instructional time available during school hours. Teachers who fail to spend the outside time to do such planning, training, coaching, and feedback with paraeducators report that they are dissatisfied with the performance of the paraeducators with whom they work.

Yet, a better arrangement is possible. Think of it this way. If 200% of the instructional time of a teacher is available because of the paraeducator, then why can't some of that time become joint meeting time to conduct the training, coaching, feedback, and communication functions of supervision? Students could still get 180% of what they would have gotten with only a teacher, and teachers and paraeducators use school hours to perform necessary functions. Conceptually, it makes sense. Of course, in practice, it means that the building schedule has to be constructed with common planning time in mind.

Covey (1989) discussed two important concepts that affect the lives of all school professionals. Administrators can help teachers and other service providers manage their time well by guiding them to understand these two concepts.

Sphere of Influence. The first concept is that of sphere of influence. The lesson is for the individual to determine those things that are within his or her circle of influence and those that are outside the sphere. To worry about things that are not within the sphere of influence wastes time and energy. To plan for, organize, and work on those things that are within the circle of influence enhances productivity. Knowing the difference is the most difficult part. Too often, teachers believe that the work the paraeducator does is outside their spheres of influence. It certainly does not have to be outside teachers' spheres of influence, and, in fact, it should be well within it. It is important for teachers to understand that being proactively engaged in orienting, training, planning for, and directing the work of paraeducators keeps them working within their legitimate sphere of influence.

Self-Management. The second concept is self-management. Self-management differs from time management in that it considers the value or worth of doing or not doing things first and then when they should be done, as opposed to merely figuring out when or how to do them. Teachers are notorious for assuming that they have to do all the tasks associated with teaching and they suffer significant amounts of stress when they are unable to meet their own expectations.

Self-management depends on an individual's ability to employ habits that enhance his or her productivity and effectiveness. The first habit is that of thinking ahead to the goals or outcomes one wants and is followed closely by being proactive in planning and organizing to achieve the goal. Teachers may fail to understand how goal setting and proactive organization can enhance their own effectiveness while improving their use of paraeducator skills and time.

CHAPTER SUMMARY

Employing paraeducators to provide instructional support to students changes the role of the classroom teacher or consulting teacher. While it increases the professional status of teachers, it requires substantial time to be spent on supervision. While supervisory responsibilities may be shared among professionals in a program, grade level, or building, additional time is required. Time is always a problem for teachers who have many simultaneous demands to fulfill. Supervision serves to limit the amount of time teachers can spend instructing students, but in spite of that, there are many good reasons for teachers to supervise. One way to alleviate the time crunch is for teachers to work smarter—meaning that they must delegate appropriate tasks to paraeducators while taking care to maintain responsibility for the outcomes.

4 Recruiting and Hiring Paraeducators

PROBLEMS AND SOLUTIONS FOR RECRUITING HIGHLY QUALIFIED APPLICANTS FOR PARAEDUCATOR POSITIONS

Recruiting and hiring highly qualified, capable people for paraeducator positions has become increasingly difficult. There are numerous reasons for this. By exploring these reasons and taking proactive steps to minimize them, administrators and teachers can recruit and hire the very best employees for the paraeducator positions in the school.

Possible Barriers to Recruiting and Hiring Highly Qualified Paraeducators

The first four potential barriers consist of a constellation of features of the job itself. These features—low pay, part-time status, poor benefits, and few promotion opportunities—may be unattractive to highly qualified, capable applicants.

The last two barriers—lack of preemployment training and poor visibility—relate to the lack of support systems for recruiting qualified applicants. There is little support for you, as a district or building-level administrator or teacher, to recruit qualified individuals. There are two main reasons for the lack of support. Like the job features, there are ways of minimizing the effects these deficiencies in the support system have on your hiring process.

Low Pay

The paraeducator position is often the lowest paid position in the school district. Those who hold paraeducator positions often earn less than the attendance secretary, the grounds maintenance personnel, and other support personnel. Sometimes, service jobs in the surrounding community pay more than the school pays for an entry-level position.

Part-Time Status

Paraeducator positions are often part-time, offering as few as 12 hours per week. Even when the position is a full-time position, there are few opportunities to make overtime pay at a higher rate. Thus, there are few opportunities for the individual to improve his or her overall income.

Poor Benefits

The position may not offer the option of purchasing group health care or insurance benefits. For some families the availability of health insurance is more important than the pay.

Few Promotion Opportunities

Paraeducator positions are often dead-end jobs. If no career ladder exists, the paraeducator has no hope of reaching a higher status or pay level. Therefore, some applicants may consider the position as a temporary job or a stopover while they search for a better job.

Lack of Preemployment Training

There are few college or university programs that prepare people for paraeducator positions. Unlike teachers, who may be first recruited by college and university preparation programs and then prepared for their roles, the entire burden for recruiting paraeducators falls on the district.

Poor Visibility

The position is not widely understood, so potential applicants may not know of the existence of such a position and may be even less certain of what the job entails. While everyone has experience with teachers, not everyone knows what paraeducators do. Therefore, it's not likely that applicants will come knocking at your door.

For all these reasons, and in places where the economy is strong and jobs abound, there may be few applicants for paraeducator positions. A small applicant pool may lead to employing people who are not well suited to the job or it may lead to unfilled positions. Throughout the 1990s, many school districts reported unfilled positions well into the school year.

Minimizing the Barriers and Capitalizing on the Attractive Job Features

Despite the barriers associated with recruiting and hiring capable people, the paraeducator position is of great interest to some highly capable people. Some paraeducators have stayed in their positions for many years in spite of job features that include low pay, limited hours, poor benefits, and lack of promotion possibilities. In addition, some long-time paraeducators report that they considered it a temporary job when they first started, but they stayed in their positions for more than 20 years because there were job features they really liked. Successful recruitment and hiring of paraeducators depends on our ability to capitalize on the job features that are most attractive to paraeducator job applicants and to minimize the effects of barriers.

Job Features That Paraeducators Find Attractive

Children. The most significant job feature that schools have to offer potential paraeducator employees is working with children. Service or other entry-level jobs in retail, fast-food, recreation, or the home health care industries just don't have that very attractive feature. Paraeducators who have stayed in their positions for a long time report that they believe their work with children is important and that the children and their families have high respect for the work they do. Some paraeducators report that they took their position because they discovered the joy of working with children when they became parents themselves. Others say that they want to work in their son or daughter's school to be close to their child and to experience their child's world. Many paraeducators who work in special education do so because they have a family member with a disability and understand the needs of persons with disabilities.

Location. Long-time paraeducators also report that they like the location of their jobs. They tend to live in the neighborhood or community in which the school is located and therefore have a very short commute. This translates into tangible benefits when you consider the costs associated with commuting time, vehicle purchase and maintenance, gas, and insurance.

Schedule. While abbreviated work hours and the lack of work during school holidays and summers is a problem for some paraeducators, for others it is an attractive job feature. The schedule is highly compatible with child rearing because it allows the parent to be home when the children are out of school.

Respect. Although there are numerous reports from paraeducators that their positions are not respected, those that have stayed in the position for a long time say that respect is a significant reason why they stay. Long-time paraeducators report that they get respect from administrators, teachers, parents, and students.

When asked to define respect, these paraeducators say that administrators and teachers have provided specific job descriptions and are clear in their directions and guidance. They report that they get training to do the tasks they are asked to do. They say that they feel that they are supported and that they are an important and recognized part of the school and the staff. They say that they hold their heads high in their community because they work at the school.

Principals play an important role in supporting and encouraging respect for paraeducators among the teachers and other members of the school community.

Opportunity to Contribute to the Community. A job feature entirely unrelated to money is based on altruism. Many people want to give something of themselves to others and working as a paraeducator is one important way to contribute meaningfully to the lives of children. In the schools that serve military personnel, retired military personnel often seek paraeducator positions as a way of returning something to the system that served their own children. In other communities, people who have retired from other careers consider it a form of honorable and pleasurable community service.

Opportunity to Explore Careers in Education. Some young people take paraeducator positions to explore the possibilities of pursuing a career in education. For them, working in a school provides firsthand knowledge of how the various school professionals engage with students, the type of work they do, their working conditions, and more. In some places, working as a paraeducator six hours a day is compatible with college coursework taken in the afternoon or at night. It enhances the meaning of students' coursework because they see the applications of theories and pedagogical concepts every day. It takes the guesswork out of choosing a major and eliminates the likelihood that they will find themselves unsuited to their choice of career at the end of their degree program—a sad outcome for some people who have completed traditional teacher preparation programs where they don't enter the classroom until the end of their programs.

When a job opening is posted, it is worthwhile to highlight the features that other successful paraeducators have found attractive and rewarding. Highly qualified and capable applicants may also be attracted to your position because of these features. It may also be worthwhile to try to hire a person at the higher end of the hourly wage range. You are more likely to find the candidate you want to hire among the pool of applicants if you do so.

ADVERTISING THE POSITION

Traditional Postings

Paraeducator positions are generally advertised according to the policies of the school or district. Traditional means of posting positions include district job bulletins, newspaper ads, and recorded phone messages. Newer means include Web site and community television listings. However, these advertisements share the characteristic that the potential applicant must come to the site seeking job information and application materials. When these means fail to attract a sufficient applicant pool, other recruitment methods become important.

Principals and teachers play a vital role in recruiting, hiring, and assigning the right people in paraeducator positions. Even in districts where personnel functions are highly centralized, there remains an important role for the building-level administrator and the teaching staff in the recruitment of suitable applicants for positions. They are always on the lookout for people who already spend time near children. There are two additional ways administrators and teachers can seek good applicants.

Word of Mouth

Word of mouth can be successfully used when you have satisfactory employees in paraeducator positions, when those people live in the community served by the school, and when they know the specifics of the position being advertised. Rely on current employees to spread the word that there is a position open. For example, Ms. Stimson, an elementary special education teacher, talked with each of the paraeducators in her program and mentioned that there would be openings in the fall. One paraeducator, Michelle, mentioned that her daughter, Christy, would graduate from high school in May and would live at home while she attended a nearby college. Michelle thought that Christy might be a good applicant if the work schedule and her college class schedule could be coordinated.

Renee, another paraeducator in the same school, mentioned the openings to her bowling teammates and parishioners at her church. As a result, there were several qualified job applicants for the positions.

Active Scouting for Quality Applicants

Sometimes the principal or teachers have the opportunity to seek applicants as they observe people who work in other parts of the school. Ms. Arden, a high school principal in California, observed a food services worker in the cafeteria during the school's summer program and was impressed with how she interacted with students. She knew that the ability to interact well with students was important to a special education paraeducator position. After that initial contact, the applicant followed the district application process.

Sometimes we can recruit applicants from people who are not currently employed by the school, but who have interest there. At Bell Middle School, Mr. French recruited the parent volunteer that coordinated the schoolwide magazine sale to apply for a half-time position as supervisor for the girls' locker room. Ms. Tucker invited her neighbor, Marla, to apply for a position as a designated paraeducator for a child with autism who would be in her kindergarten class in the fall. Marla had a child in the same class and was concurrently earning her master's degree in educational psychology. Ms. Tucker knew she would be able to work well with Marla and that Marla would be a qualified applicant. Ms. Pope, a third- and fourth-grade team leader, visited the high school Future Teachers of America club to find a part-time clerical assistant for her team. Heather, a senior, came to work at 1:45 when her classes finished and worked until 4:00 every day, preparing and producing instructional materials for the teachers.

Administrators, teachers, and paraeducators who spread information about job openings by word of mouth and through active recruitment must remember that they should never imply that they are guaranteeing a position to the people they recruit. They must remain somewhat neutral in the process because the hiring process must be legally conducted in ways that conform to the equal-opportunity and nondiscrimination policies of the district. The Paraeducator Recruitment Possibilities Worksheet (Table 4.1) provides a reminder of many recruitment possibilities.

Table 4.1   Paraeducator Recruitment Possibilities Worksheet

✓	Have you scouted for:
	People who already work for the district?
	a) Food services workers?
	b) Bus drivers?
	c) Campus supervisors?
	d) Clerical personnel?
	Volunteers?
	e) Parents of children in the building?
	f) Members of PTA or other parent advisory committees?
	g) Parents of children in a nearby school?
	h) Senior citizens who live in the neighborhood?
	Community contacts?
	i) Neighbors, friends, or relatives of current paraeducators?
	j) Neighbors, friends, or relatives of teachers?
	k) Neighbors, friends, or relatives of the school clerical staff?
	Former or current students?
	l) Students who previously worked as peer assistants in special education programs, physical education, or computer classes (particularly in secondary schools)?
	m) High school students who can earn work-study credit for working with younger children?

SCREENING THE APPLICANTS

Preemployment Preparation

Rarely are we able to recruit applicants who have formal preparation for the position of paraeducator. There are community college, technical college, and occupational programs that prepare people for such positions, but they are small and widely scattered, and cannot begin to meet the personnel demand. When you are able to attract graduates of such programs, however, they may bring added value to the applicant pool. Program graduates

- Can substantiate the coursework they've taken with a transcript

- Are likely to have letters of recommendation

- May have completed a practicum or field experience in which a teacher or principal served as supervisor and provided a skill evaluation

Table 4.2 includes a partial listing of programs that prepare paraeducators. Local yellow pages may also contain listings of programs that you might contact to find applicants who have some preemployment preparation.

Of course, there is no standardized curriculum for preemployment preparation of paraeducators, so you cannot assume that applicants who have completed programs have been prepared with the same level of rigor or have covered similar material.

One way to assess the quality of preemployment training courses for special education paraeducator position applicants is to compare the program requirements to a list of standards for entry-level paraeducators compiled and validated by the Council for Exceptional Children (CEC) in conjunction with the National Education Association (NEA) and the American Federation of Teachers (AFT). This list is contained in Table 4.3 and may be used to compare the standards for knowledge and skills to the coursework required in the preemployment training program for paraeducators.

Prerequisite Interpersonal Skills

Whether a person has completed a preservice program or not, there are numerous interpersonal skills that make the difference between a successful paraeducator and one that performs unsatisfactorily. First, effective oral communication skills are necessary to most paraeducator positions. Without effective listening and speaking skills, a paraeducator may be unable to follow directions or bring information back to the teacher about student behavior and progress.

The level of written communication skills necessary may vary by position. For example, a paraeducator who serves children with learning disabilities may be called upon to help them organize, compose, and write sentences, paragraphs, essays, or other written genre. If the paraeducator has poor written communication skills, it may not be possible for that person to provide the necessary supports to the student. On the other hand, if that same paraeducator was working with young children for whom speaking and reading were the primary tasks, a lack of sophisticated writing skills may not be detrimental.

The level of mathematical skill may also vary by position. Paraeducators working with younger children may not need much knowledge of algebra or geometry, but those who will be assigned to support students in middle school and high school level mathematics courses probably will. It is important to specify the kinds of skills you are seeking in the posted job description.

Personal Qualities and Characteristics of Good Applicants

While applicants for paraeducator positions may come from various sources and walks of life, there are some common characteristics that make an

Table 4.2   Examples of Community College Programs That Prepare Paraeducators

College	Program Name	Program Outcome	Type of Preparation	Contact Information
Kirkwood Community College Cedar Rapids, IA	Iowa Paraeducator Certification Program	Level I – Generalist Certificate Level II – Area of Concentration Level II – Advanced AA Degree or 62 approved credits	Special education Early childhood education Limited English proficiency Career and transition	Susan Simon Brenton Hall/Disability Services 6301 Kirkwood Boulevard Cedar Rapids, IA 52406 (319) 398-4510 ssimon@kirkwood.cc.ia.us www.kirkwood.cc.ia.us/socialsciences /careeroption/madiff/para_dia.htm
Community College of Denver Denver, CO	Paraeducator Certificate Program	Paraeducator Certificate AA Degree	Special education Literacy Bilingual education	Christine Tanguay Program Director Community College of Denver–North 6221 Downing St. Denver, CO 80216 (303) 289-2243 x 117 Christine.Tanguay@ccd.cccoes.edu
Whatcom Community College Bellingham, WA	Educational Paraprofessional Program	AA Degree	K-12 schools	Sally Holloway Coordinator of Education Programs Whatcom Community College 237 West Kellogg Road Bellingham, WA 98226 shollowa@whatcom.ctc.edu
Quinebaug Valley Community College Willimantic, CT	Educational Paraprofessional Program	Certificate	K-12 schools (most course-work is in early childhood)	Mary Romney Willimantic Center 729 Main St., Willimantic, CT, 06226 (860) 423-1824
Cloud Community College Concordia, KS	⇧ Early Childhood Paraprofessional ⇧ Infant/Toddler Teacher ⇧ Child Care Teacher ⇧ Teacher Assistant		Assistant, head teacher, or director in a preschool or child care center, in the home or facility outside the home	Misty Dawn Durfee-Elder 2221 Campus Dr. PO Box 1002 Concordia, KS 66901 (785) 243-1435 (888) 527-8680

Table 4.2 continued

College	Program Name	Program Outcome	Type of Preparation	Contact Information
Walla Walla Community College Walla Walla, WA	Education Paraprofessional	Certificate and AA degree options	Prepares students for paraeducator and instructional assistant roles in preschool, primary and secondary schools	Melinda Brennan Melinda.Brennan@po.ww.cc.wa.us (360) 527-4237
Western Wisconsin Technical College West Salem, WI	Instructional Assistant Technical Diploma Program	Technical diploma		Leanne Healy Western Wisconsin Technical College (608) 789-6288 healyl@western.tec.wi.us
Montessori Education Centers Associated	Paraprofessional Program	Certificate of Attendance	Paraprofessionals in Montessori programs for children 3–6 years old	Montessori Education Centers 5728 Virginia Street Clarendon Hills, IL 60514 (630) 654-0151 MECA1Seton@aol.com

Table 4.3   CEC Knowledge (K) and Skills (S) for Beginning Special Education Paraeducators

Standard 1. Foundations
K1.   Purposes of programs for individuals with exceptional learning needs
K2.   Basic instructional terminology regarding students, programs, roles, and instructional activities
Standard 2. Development and Characteristics of Learners
K1.   Effects an exceptional condition(s) can have on an individual's life
Standard 3. Individual Learning Differences
K1.   Rights and responsibilities of families and children as they relate to individual learning needs
K2.   Indicators of abuse and neglect
S1.   Demonstrate sensitivity to the diversity of individuals and families
Standard 4. Instructional Strategies
K1.   Basic instructional and remedial strategies and materials
K2.   Basic technologies appropriate to individuals with exceptional learning needs
S1.   Use strategies, equipment, materials, and technologies, as directed, to accomplish instructional objectives
S2.   Assist in adapting instructional strategies and materials as directed
S3.   Use strategies as directed to facilitate effective integration into various settings
S4.   Use strategies that promote the learner's independence as directed
S5.   Use strategies as directed to increase the individual's independence and confidence
Standard 5. Learning Environments and Social Interactions
K1.   Demands of various learning environments
K2.   Rules and procedural safeguards regarding the management of behaviors of individuals with exceptional learning needs
S1.   Establish and maintain rapport with learners
S2.   Use universal precautions and assist in maintaining a safe, healthy learning environment

Table 4.3 continued

S3.	Use strategies for managing behavior as directed
S4.	Use strategies as directed, in a variety of settings, to assist in the development of social skills
Standard 6. Language	
K1.	Characteristics of appropriate communication with stakeholders
Standard 7. Instructional Planning	
S1.	Follow written plans, seeking clarification as needed
S2.	Prepare and organize materials to support teaching and learning as directed
Standard 8. Assessment	
K1.	Rationale for assessment
S1.	Demonstrate basic collection techniques as directed
S2.	Make and document objective observations as directed
Standard 9. Professional and Ethical Practice	
K1.	Ethical practices for confidential communication about individuals with exceptional learning needs
K2.	Personal cultural biases and differences that affect one's ability to work with others
S1.	Perform responsibilities as directed in a manner consistent with laws and policies
S2.	Follow instructions of the professional
S3.	Demonstrate problem solving, flexible thinking, conflict management techniques, and analysis of personal strengths and preferences
S4.	Act as a role model for individuals with exceptional learning needs.
S5.	Demonstrate commitment to assisting learners in achieving their highest potential.
S6.	Demonstrate the ability to separate personal issues from one's responsibilities as a paraeducator.
S7.	Maintain a high level of competence and integrity.
S8.	Exercise objective and prudent judgment.

Table 4.3 continued

S9.	Demonstrate proficiency in academic skills, including oral and written communication.
S10.	Engage in activities to increase one's own knowledge and skills.
S11.	Engage in self-assessment.
S12.	Accept and use constructive feedback.
S13.	Demonstrate ethical practices as guided by the CEC Code of Ethics and other standards and policies.
Standard 10. Collaboration	
K1.	Common concerns of families and individuals with exceptional learning needs.
K2.	Roles of stakeholders in planning an individualized program.
S1.	Assist in collection and providing objective, accurate information to professionals.
S2.	Collaborate with stakeholders as directed.
S3.	Foster respectful and beneficial relationships.
S4.	Participate as directed in conferences as members of the educational team.
S5.	Function in a manner that demonstrates a positive regard for the distinctions between roles and responsibilities of paraeducators and those of professionals.

SOURCE: CEC Performance-based Standards: Paraeducators. Retrieved from www.cec.sped.org/ps/perf_based_stds/paraeducators_03-12-01 on May 24, 2002.

applicant viable. When teachers talk about the characteristics of the best paraeducators they list flexibility, willingness to take direction and listen, and a genuine affinity for doing things with kids and being around kids. They also recognize that paraeducators who take initiative, show responsibility, and recognize what needs to be done are more valuable than those who sit back and wait to be told what to do in every situation. In special education programs, teachers look for sensitivity to students whose academic, social, and physical needs are different from those of the typical student.

While sensitivity and affection for students are important qualities, teachers have grave concerns about applicants who need to be needed. Sometimes applicants whose personal needs are so great are likely to over-mother or smother students with their good intentions once they are employed. For example, a one-to-one paraeducator working with a child who has physical needs may need to provide a lot of physical support to the child, but must also be able to step back and allow the child to develop independent skills in self-care.

Some paraeducator positions require strong organizational skills or personality styles that thrive on methodical, almost compulsive work habits. For example, a paraeducator hired to manage special education paperwork in a high school needs to be absolutely thorough about getting every piece of paper signed, dated, and filed on time. People with habitual behaviors often work well in such positions. Finding the right candidate is the key and you are more likely to do so if you put the preferred characteristics in the posted job description.

Application Procedures

Application Questions

Federal and state laws prohibit discrimination in employment based on disability, race, creed, color, sex, religion, national origin, or ancestry. In most districts, the standard application forms have been carefully analyzed to ensure compliance with nondiscrimination and equal-opportunity laws. Sometimes building-level personnel are cautioned not to change the standard application forms or procedures out of concern that a lack of knowledge could cause discriminatory mistakes.

However, it is legal to supplement standard application forms with job-related questions that pertain specifically to the open position. For example, questions about ancestry, first language, national origin of parents or spouse, date of arrival in the United States, port of entry, how long the applicant has been a U.S. resident, or maiden name of wife or mother may not be asked. However, if a particular position requires the paraeducator to speak Arabic to students whose primary language is Arabic, translate letters to parents and families, translate instructional materials into Arabic, or serve as a live interpreter during face-to-face meetings between speakers of English and speakers of Arabic, then it is both reasonable and lawful to include questions about the applicant's ability to perform such tasks on the application form and during interviews.

Performance Tasks

It is also legal to ask an applicant to perform job-specific skills as part of the application and interview process. In some districts it is standard procedure to require a test of basic academic skills, for example. It would also be legal and appropriate to ask a person to take a computer test, to perform a translation, or to write a paragraph as long as the task reflects an actual job requirement.

Hiring Interviews

Interviews serve two purposes. First, interviews provide the opportunity to ask applicants about their abilities to perform job functions. Second, they permit current employees to determine whether the personal traits and preferences of the applicant make a good match with the situation. It is good practice to involve those employees who will work most closely with the new person. When that is impossible, the interviewer may want to use a device such as the work style and preference inventory (see Tables 5.3, 5.4, and 5.5 in Chapter 5) to note the similarities and differences in work styles and preferences of those who will work closely together.

Inquiring About Preferences and Work Styles

It is always legal in application forms and in interviews to ask applicants about their own work styles and work preferences. The answers or responses may be used to determine whether there is a good match between the applicant and the work situation and among the people who will work together. It would be useful to have the teacher or other team members fill out the personal work styles and preferences form prior to the interview and then have each applicant do the same at the interview.

Ability to Perform Duties

It is also legal and acceptable to ask an applicant about his or her ability to perform specific job duties. Of course, using a vaguely worded list won't help much. But if the teacher has taken the time to specify in some level of detail the types of tasks the paraeducator is expected to do, that list can be used to structure the interview protocol. The Master List of Tasks and Duties (see Table 5.5 in Chapter 5) may be used to create a complete listing of all the specific tasks that need to be completed in a particular grade level or program. It is wise to include all tasks—even those that are not so pleasant.

For example, Ms. Carroll teaches secondary students with significant disabilities. Some of her students need to have their diapers changed. She always asks paraeducator position applicants whether they are comfortable with changing the diapers of 17-year-old students. When an applicant blanches and turns away during the interview, she knows that the applicant would not be a good candidate for the position. She would rather continue interviewing to find a person who is likely to stay and do the job than hire someone who will get a rude awakening on the first day of employment and resign. She knows through experience that it wastes her time and energy to orient a new paraeducator who quits after three days on the job. She knows that it is better to spend time up front interviewing well than spend time training new hires that leave.

Giving Enough Information to the Applicant

The interview is a perfect time to provide ample information about the nature of the job to the applicant. Including a tour of the building and introductions to coworkers and students takes a few minutes more but may pay off in your ability to hire the best-qualified applicants.

Following Up on References

It is legal to follow up on references and recommendations with people who the applicant has named as references. It is also legal to pursue references who the applicant has not named, but who may have information about the applicant's job performance in a previous position. If you know someone at a place where the applicant has previously been employed, or if you have trusted colleagues in the neighborhood, they are possible sources of information about how well-suited the applicant is to the position. There are several questions you can ask of references that provide the maximum information. The following list contains examples of legal and ethical questions for references.

- In what capacity have you known the applicant?

- Can you describe the applicant's work performance?

- What responsibilities did the applicant have?

- What are the applicant's strengths and weaknesses?

- What was the working relationship between this applicant and his or her peers?

- What are the job responsibilities for the position? Do you think the applicant could perform them?

- Why did the applicant leave your employ?

- Would you rehire this applicant?

CHAPTER SUMMARY

Recruiting and hiring qualified, capable people for paraeducator positions is difficult, but important. While the paraeducator position is inherently difficult and poorly paid, there are several positive features that can be used to attract good applicants. Active scouting often leads to a deep applicant pool. Screening of applicants for prior education, employment experience, and personal qualities saves time in interviews. It is legal and ethical to ask applicants about their ability to perform tasks required of the position. It is also valuable to give applicants an overview of the position and the school so they will understand the nature of the work and the workplace.

Finally, following up on references provided by the applicant is an important part of the process. This step helps eliminate the possibility of hiring someone who has had employment difficulties in the past.

5 Starting Off on the Right Foot: Providing Orientation

Gretchen came home from her first day on the job as a teaching assistant in the nearby elementary school very tired and a little upset. She stopped by her neighbor's house and asked, "Do you think this is right?" She explained her question.

> I got to school early because it was my first day, expecting that they'd show me around and help me get started. Instead, the teacher, Arlis, had just come out of a meeting and was rushing around doing other things. She showed me the room I'd be in, and then she told me that students would arrive in about 20 minutes. I asked what I'd be doing with students, and Arlis responded by saying that there was some math stuff in the top drawer of the file cabinet that I could use. I didn't know where to put my lunch or my purse, or what my schedule would be. I wondered where the bathroom was. But then the reality hit me that I had to think of something to do with a group of students in just a few minutes. So, I dug in the drawer and began to figure out a plan. I survived the day, but I don't know how much the kids learned.

Her neighbor responded with a serious question, "Is this a real job?" Gretchen laughed as she responded, "It felt more like a test . . . like they were testing me to see if I could figure out where things were and what I was supposed to do."

This job is a test...

It is only a test...

If it were a real job...

You would have been given instructions

on where to go and what to do.

—Kent Gerlach

Strengthening the Partnership

ORIENTATION FOR NEWLY EMPLOYED PARAEDUCATORS

There are some practices that will make the first day on a new job go smoothly for both the paraeducator and the teacher. The first day on a new job is a critical time for paraprofessionals. It is only reasonable to expect an initial orientation prior to the first day. Table 5.1 lists the five components of paraeducator orientation that should occur prior to student contact, the five components that should occur during the first week of employment, and the two additional components that should be completed during the first month. The table is presented as a checklist on which the supervisor can check and initial or date when each component is completed. It also suggests that orientation is a process that consists of three stages: getting acquainted, establishing the supervisory relationship, and keeping the momentum.

Get Acquainted

Orientation to Surroundings

First, common courtesy demands that newly employed paraeducators should be introduced to the other people who work in the school. If the school is large and staff numerous, then prioritize the introductions. First, plan to introduce the paraeducator to office staff, custodial staff, health care staff, and safety and security personnel. This is easily accomplished at the same time that the paraeducator is touring the building and learning the locations of exits, classrooms, offices, supply rooms, workrooms, lunchrooms, libraries, gyms, and so on. In short, the paraeducator should be shown the locations of all rooms, spaces, and equipment they may need to use. Time spent up front orienting the new employee saves time later when tasks need to be accomplished and there is little time to learn the location of necessary items.

Policy and Procedure Orientation

Second, the paraeducator should be provided with any and all written policies and procedures used in the building. At the minimum such written infor-

Table 5.1   Orientation Components Checklist

Get Acquainted (Before Student Contact)	Establish the Supervisory Relationship (First 5 Days on the Job)	Keep the Momentum (First Month)
⇨ Introductions to office, safety/security, health care and physical plant employees, some teachers	⇨ Introductions to all teachers, other paraeducators, library and media staff	⇨ Complete the plan for acquisition of new skills needed on the job, adding those that weren't apparent during role clarification
⇨ Tour of the building	⇨ Getting acquainted interview	
⇨ Written safety and emergency procedures	⇨ Work style preferences analysis/comparison to all supervising professionals	
⇨ School calendar, routines, procedures, general expectations, protocols for absences, substitutes, etc.	⇨ Role clarification and specific job description based on program needs and paraeducator skills, noting immediate training needed	⇨ Complete all introductions, making sure even the itinerant related services providers have been introduced
⇨ Confidentiality, student rights	⇨ Program purpose(s), organization, operation	

mation should include emergency and safety procedures; school rules, routines, and standard procedures; the school calendar; the building-level schedule; phone numbers and addresses of fellow employees; and protocols for reporting absences, requesting substitutes, and getting information about emergency school closures. Many schools have developed a handbook that contains vital information about safety issues such as fire drills, emergency warning systems, and playground or assembly rules. It may not be necessary to create a separate handbook or packet for paraeducators if a schoolwide handbook already exists. In fact, it makes most sense to provide the same written information to both paraeducators and professionals.

Confidentiality

Third, it is imperative that the orientation that occurs prior to student contact includes information about the privacy rights of all students, based on the Federal Educational Rights and Privacy Act (FERPA) and other laws such as IDEA. The average person taking a position as a paraeducator will never have been exposed to this information. The opportunities to talk "out of school" about students, staff, and families of students will be ample—even on the first day of employment. Yet, it always seems to come as a surprise to new para-educators, who never expect that people will ask. Nor do they realize how eager they will be to talk about their new job! Most of all, they don't anticipate how difficult it is to think of something to say that is both tactful and ethical when the temptation arises to gossip about teachers, paraeducators, or other school personnel. It is even more difficult for them when they are asked about students. People in communities want to know about each other and about their neighbors' children. It is crucial to provide the new employee with guidelines for keeping information about students confidential and maintaining the highest ethical standards. In addition, supervisors should provide some easy-to-use responses to the new employee to use whenever others, who have no right to know confidential information, ask questions. Table 5.2 provides a sample of some possible questions a new employee might expect and some responses the

Table 5.2   Rehearsed Responses to Requests for Confidential Information

Possible Request	Possible Responses
"I heard you're working at the school. . . . Is that third-grade teacher as mean as everyone says?"	"I'm an employee at the school now, I can't talk about my colleagues that way." or "Employees aren't allowed to talk about one another outside of school, sorry."
"Who's the funny looking kid that flaps his hands all the time?"	"Student information is confidential to everyone but his parents and teachers." or "Sorry, I can't talk about kids outside of school."
"What's the scoop on Gail . . . I heard her husband . . . ?"	"Gail's my fellow employee as well as my friend now, I can't discuss her private life."
"What's wrong with Suzanna?"	"Student information is protected by law. I'd be breaking the law if I spoke about any student outside of school."
"I heard Jason is doing better with that new special ed teacher."	"Jason's progress is confidential. It's not okay for me to discuss it."
"Is Tanya in the special reading class?"	"Placement of students is a confidential matter. We're not allowed to speak about student placements outside of school."

paraeducator may want to rehearse ahead of time. A few minutes spent rehearsing some responses during the initial orientation can protect the rights of both students and school employees.

Introductions

New paraeducators should have a structured opportunity to get to know their fellow school employees. On the first day, or at least within the first week, it is reasonable to introduce a new paraeducator to the people with whom he or she will be working directly. Of special concern are the teachers and other para-professionals with whom he or she will come in contact right away. For example, a paraeducator may accompany a middle school student to academic classes. Without prior introductions, an awkward situation arises when the paraeducator shows up with the student. Experienced paraeducators may handle the situation by introducing themselves and explaining their role to the teacher. New paraeducators are likely to assume that the classroom teacher knows who they are and why they are there. This assumption, of course, is not likely to be accurate. Real damage may be done to a student's status in school when no one remembers to introduce the adults that work on his or her behalf.

In addition, a paraeducator may be asked questions about students. For them to provide information to those that have a right to know and avoid making the mistakes of breaching confidentiality, paraeducators must know who is and who isn't connected with a particular student. An extended checklist of people in the school that a paraeducator may need to know is shown in Table 5.3.

Establish the Supervisory Relationship

Structured Initial Conversation

Getting to know the individual or team that will provide supervision is of primary importance to the paraeducator. One way for school professionals and newly employed paraeducators to get to know one another is to have a structured initial conversation. Table 5.4 contains some possible questions that can help two people get acquainted during a structured conversation. Professionals may create other questions that will help them get to know the new person. The structured conversation is not meant to replace a hiring interview. Rather, it is meant to occur at the beginning of employment to help newly employed paraeducators gain knowledge of their fellow workers and to help team members get to know one another.

Work Style and Preferences Analysis

The next step is to conduct a work style and preferences analysis. To conduct this analysis, use the worksheets shown in Tables 5.5 through 5.7. The first worksheet, Professional Work Style (Table 5.5), requires the professional to reflect upon his or her own preferences in order to communicate them to the newly employed paraeducator. The paraeducator version, titled Paraeducator Work Style (Table 5.6), allows the paraeducator to clarify his or her preferences in order to communicate them as well.

Table 5.3 Introductions Checklist for Newly Employed Paraeducators

Office	Names	Health Care	Names	Physical Plant	Names
⇧ Secretary	⇧	⇧ School nurse	⇧	⇧ Custodians	⇧
⇧ Attendance clerk	⇧	⇧ Health room clerk	⇧	⇧ Building engineers/managers	⇧
⇧ Financial clerk	⇧	⇧	⇧	⇧ Grounds managers	⇧
⇧ Clerical assistants	⇧	⇧	⇧	⇧	⇧
		⇧	⇧		⇧
		⇧	⇧		

Safety/Security	Names	Library	Names	Related Services	Names
⇧ Lunchroom monitors	⇧	⇧ Media specialist	⇧	⇧ School psychologist	⇧
⇧ Playground monitors	⇧	⇧ Media/library paraprofessionals	⇧	⇧ Social worker	⇧
⇧ Bus loading monitors	⇧	⇧	⇧	⇧ Physical therapist	⇧
⇧ Security guards	⇧	⇧	⇧	⇧ Occupational therapist	⇧
	⇧	⇧	⇧	⇧ Speech-language pathologist	⇧
	⇧	⇧	⇧		⇧

Classroom Teachers	Names	Special Subject Teachers	Names	Paraeducators	Names
	⇧	⇧ Art	⇧		⇧
	⇧	⇧ Music	⇧		⇧
	⇧	⇧ PE	⇧		⇧
	⇧	⇧ Home Ec	⇧		⇧
	⇧	⇧ Shop	⇧		⇧
	⇧	⇧ Special education	⇧		⇧
	⇧	⇧ Bilingual education	⇧		⇧
	⇧	⇧ Title I	⇧		⇧

Table 5.4   Getting Acquainted: Paraeducator Structured Conversation Questions

1. Why have you decided to work as a paraeducator/teacher?

2. What are your recreational activities or hobbies?

3. Which of your teachers made the biggest positive impact on you?

4. What other skills do you have that we might incorporate into the classroom?

5. What is your understanding of this position?

6. What do you think are the goals of education?

7. What other teams have you participated on? Sports? Work?

8. What talents and skills do you bring to the team?

9. How do you think teams function best?

10. How can we ensure that we will work well together?

Table 5.5 Professional Work Style

Directions: *Circle the number that indicates your level of agreement or disagreement with each statement.*

	Disagree				Agree
1. I supervise paraeducators closely.	1	2	3	4	5
2. I like a flexible work schedule.	1	2	3	4	5
3. I let paraeducators know exactly what is expected	1	2	3	4	5
4. I provide (or at least determine) all the materials that will be used.	1	2	3	4	5
5. I provide a written work schedule.	1	2	3	4	5
6. I expect the paraeducator to think ahead to the next task.	1	2	3	4	5
7. I determine the instructional methods that will be used.	1	2	3	4	5
8. I encourage the paraeducator to try new activities independently.	1	2	3	4	5
9. I give explicit directions for each task	1	2	3	4	5
10. I always do several things at one time	1	2	3	4	5
11. I like working with paraeducators that willingly take on new challenges.	1	2	3	4	5
12. I like taking care of details.	1	2	3	4	5
13. I require the paraeducator to be very punctual	1	2	3	4	5
14. I like to get frequent feedback on how I can improve as a supervisor	1	2	3	4	5
15. I like to bring problems out in the open	1	2	3	4	5
16. I like to give frequent performance feedback to the paraeducator	1	2	3	4	5
17. I like to discuss activities that do not go well	1	2	3	4	5
18. I like working with other adults	1	2	3	4	5
19. I encourage paraeducators to think for themselves	1	2	3	4	5
20. I am a morning person	1	2	3	4	5
21. I speak slowly and softly	1	2	3	4	5
22. I work best alone with little immediate interaction	1	2	3	4	5
23. I need a quiet place to work without distractions	1	2	3	4	5
24. I prefer that no one else touches my things	1	2	3	4	5
25. I prefer to work from a written plan	1	2	3	4	5

Table 5.6 Paraeducator Work Style

Directions: *Circle the number that indicates your level of agreement / disagreement with each statement.*			
		Disagree	Agree

1. I like to be supervised closely. 1 2 3 4 5
2. I like a flexible work schedule..... ....1 2 3 4 5
3. I like to know exactly what is expected. 1 2 3 4 5
4. I prefer to decide which materials to use 1 2 3 4 5
5. I like having a written work schedule.........................1 2 3 4 5
6. I need time to think ahead on the next task. 1 2 3 4 5
7. I like to determine the instructional methods I use 1 2 3 4 5
8. I like to try new activities independently.....................1 2 3 4 5
9. I like to be told how to do each task 1 2 3 4 5
10. I like to do several things at one time. 1 2 3 4 5
11. I like to take on challenges and new situations. 1 2 3 4 5
12. I like taking care of details. 1 2 3 4 5
13. I like to be very punctual 1 2 3 4 5
14. I like to give frequent feedback on
    how I prefer to be supervised 1 2 3 4 5
15. I like to bring problems out in the open.......................1 2 3 4 5
16. I like to get frequent feedback on my performance.......1 2 3 4 5
17. I like to discuss when activities do not go well 1 2 3 4 5
18. I like working with other adults 1 2 3 4 5
19. I like to think things through for myself.......................1 2 3 4 5
20. I am a morning person 1 2 3 4 5
21. I like to speak slowly and softly 1 2 3 4 5
22. I like to work alone with little immediate interaction 1 2 3 4 5
23. I need a quiet place to work without distractions 1 2 3 4 5
24. I prefer that no one else touches my things 1 2 3 4 5
25. I prefer to work from a written plan 1 2 3 4 5

To begin, the paraeducator and the professional(s) fill out the worksheets individually using the appropriate form. Then, together, the professional(s) and the paraeducator fill in the Work Style Score Comparison Sheet (Table 5.7). The score sheet is intended to be a vehicle for communication about how the two (or the team) will work together. Items where the scores vary by only a point tend to be fairly easy to discuss. Items where the score differences are greater need to be discussed further. Knowing the preferences of a newly employed paraeducator and comparing them to the preferred work style of the professional team members enables the team to start off on the right foot. Remember that the scores are not absolutes. Everyone is capable of adapting their own preferences to those of their teammates.

It is also important for all team members to recognize that style preferences are not inherently good or bad, but that they do exist. The lack of initial recognition of differences often creates a breeding ground for interpersonal problems between paraeducators and professionals. Managing differences from the start means that the team members must note differences in work style preferences, recognizing that preferences are just that—preferences. They are not flaws or personality defects, but simple likes and dislikes. And everyone is different.

Table 5.7 Work Style Score Comparison Sheet

Directions: Transfer scores from Tables 5.3 and 5.4 to this form. Examine areas of agreement and disagreement. Your combined profile is unique: there are no correct scores or combinations. Decide whether your combinations are okay or not. Have a conversation in which you strive to determine how you will proceed to work together in light of your areas of agreement and disagreement. Write out your decisions on each item that poses an area of difficulty for you.

Disagree Agree	Item Content	Disagree Agree
1 2 3 4 5	1. Closeness of supervision	1 2 3 4 5
1 2 3 4 5	2. Flexibility of work schedule	1 2 3 4 5
1 2 3 4 5	3. Preciseness of expectations	1 2 3 4 5
1 2 3 4 5	4. Decisions on which materials to use	1 2 3 4 5
1 2 3 4 5	5. Written work schedule	1 2 3 4 5
1 2 3 4 5	6. Time to think ahead on the next task	1 2 3 4 5
1 2 3 4 5	7. Decisions on instructional methods	1 2 3 4 5
1 2 3 4 5	8. Trying new activities independently	1 2 3 4 5
1 2 3 4 5	9. Specifying how to do each task	1 2 3 4 5
1 2 3 4 5	10. Doing several things at one time	1 2 3 4 5
1 2 3 4 5	11. Taking on challenges	1 2 3 4 5
1 2 3 4 5	12. Taking care of details	1 2 3 4 5
1 2 3 4 5	13. Punctuality	1 2 3 4 5
1 2 3 4 5	14. Giving and getting feedback on supervision	1 2 3 4 5
1 2 3 4 5	15. Dealing with problems out in the open	1 2 3 4 5
1 2 3 4 5	16. Giving and getting frequent feedback	1 2 3 4 5
1 2 3 4 5	17. Discussing activities that do not go well	1 2 3 4 5
1 2 3 4 5	18. Working with other adults	1 2 3 4 5
1 2 3 4 5	19. Thinking things through for myself	1 2 3 4 5
1 2 3 4 5	20. I am a morning person	1 2 3 4 5
1 2 3 4 5	21. Speak slowly and softly	1 2 3 4 5
1 2 3 4 5	22. Working alone or with little interaction	1 2 3 4 5
1 2 3 4 5	23. Quiet place to work with no distractions	1 2 3 4 5
1 2 3 4 5	24. Touching others' things	1 2 3 4 5
1 2 3 4 5	25. Working from a written plan	1 2 3 4 5

Consider what happened to Gretchen early in her first few weeks as a paraeducator (Box 5.1). No one had taken the time to have a discussion about work style preferences at the start of Gretchen's employment. She had been using the stapler on Arlis' desk because it was the only one she saw. This choice set the stage for miscommunication and mistrust on the first day, with little discussion about the nature of the job, the rules, or the styles or preferences of the individuals who would work in close proximity. Some people simply prefer that no one else touches or moves certain tools or personal effects.

Obviously, there were at least two different possible actions Gretchen and Arlis could have taken from the start. Arlis could have procured a second set of desk supplies for Gretchen and provided a small table, desk, box, or corner for her to keep them. Or, she could have told Gretchen how she felt about having to look for things and asked her from the start to take care to replace the stapler in a certain spot.

BOX 5.1.

THE STAPLER INCIDENT

Gretchen sensed that Arlis, the teacher she worked with, was irritated with her, but she didn't know why. Gretchen tried to figure out what she had done. Each day it seemed a little worse. Finally, she said something to Arlis. "Have I done something wrong?" Arlis replied with irritation in her voice, "Could you just leave my stuff alone?" Gretchen was stunned. "What stuff?" she asked. Arlis said, "Every time I reach for my stapler, you've moved it somewhere else. I hate having to look for it when I'm in a hurry and I need to staple something." Embarrassed, Gretchen mumbled, "Well, I didn't realize I was doing that, but I'll try to put it back in the same place after I use it." She walked away thinking, "What's the big deal? Who cares if the stapler is moved a little one way or the other?"

Because paraeducators and teachers work so closely, often sharing materials, supplies, and space, the opportunities to get in each other's way and to do things that irritate the other person are ample. Conducting a preferences and work style analysis, followed by a discussion of how to manage the differences, can greatly reduce the potential for conflicts to arise.

Defining the Job

The next component of orientation includes an introduction to the role of the paraeducator, to the schedule, and to the specific job duties. This orientation phase should not be unidirectional. Because paraeducator roles are somewhat negotiable (within certain legal and ethical limits), and because of the possible overlapping of responsibilities, it is most appropriate to gain some additional information about the paraeducator at this stage. The best way to obtain information about the newly employed paraeducator is to ask. In addition, throughout orientation, the new paraeducator should be encouraged to ask questions and share concerns about the position or assigned duties. Defining the job involves five basic steps.

1. *Create a task list for paraeducators.* The first step is to analyze all the tasks that need to be performed for the program to function, for students to thrive, and for the paraeducator's own needs to be met. The Master List of Tasks and Duties (Table 5.8) can be used to help professionals list all the possible duties. Professionals who work together may want to create one master list or each professional may want to create his or her own master list. Either way, such a list represents categories of tasks that typically need to be done to ensure student success at school and to maintain the program, the team relationship, the classroom, and the work climate.

Table 5.8 Master List of Tasks and Duties

Directions: *Create a master list of all the tasks you need completed for your program and students to succeed. The items in this list are merely suggestions. Feel free to revise or replace items with tasks or duties that are more relevant to your program. Specify details as needed for clarity.*

Supervision of Groups of Students

1. Assist individual students on arrival or departure (specify _____)
2. Supervise groups of students during lunch
3. Supervise groups of students during recess
4. Supervise groups of students loading and unloading buses
5. Monitor students during hall passing periods
6. Escort groups of students to bathroom, library, gym, etc.
7. Accompany students to therapy sessions, individual appointments, etc.
8. Teach appropriate social behaviors in common areas
9. Carry out behavior management
10. Participate in classroom behavioral system as directed
11. Provide reinforcement and support according to IEPs or individualized behavior plans
12. Mediate interpersonal conflicts between students
13. Provide instruction to students on how to mediate their own conflicts
14. Provide cues or prompts to students who are mediating conflicts
15. Provide physical proximity for students with behavior problems
16. Circulate in classroom to provide behavioral supports where needed
17. Enforce class and school rules
18. Assist students who are self-managing behavior (e.g., provide cues, prompts)
19. Help students develop and self-monitor organizational skills
20. Provide cues or prompts to students to use impulse and anger control strategies
21. Provide cues or prompts to students to employ specific prosocial skills
22. Teach prosocial skill lessons
23. Facilitate appropriate social interactions among students
24. Assist other students in coping with the behaviors of specific students (e.g., bullies)

Delivery of Instruction, Therapy, or Services

25. Conduct drill and practice activities (e.g., vocabulary, math facts, articulation protocols)
26. Read or repeat tests or directions to students
27. Read with students (specify techniques _____[e.g., guided oral reading, neurological impress, repeated readings, choral reading])
28. Help students complete written assignments
29. Assist students to compose original work (e.g., stories, essays, reports)
30. Tape-record stories, lessons, assignments
31. Carry out adapted instruction according to the adaptation list provided or specific directions (e.g., lesson plans, IEPs)
32. Read to students (specify _____ [e.g., text material, stories])
33. Listen to students reading orally
34. Help students work on individual projects
35. Facilitate students' active participation in cooperative groups
36. Help students select library books and reference materials
37. Help students use computers (specify purpose_____[e.g., keyboarding, drill and practice, composing written assignments, printing, finding resources on Internet)
38. Translate instruction or student responses (e.g., sign or other language)
39. Translate directions into other language for student(s) (e.g., ASL)

Table 5.8   continued

40. Translate teacher-made materials or text materials into another language
41. Use another language (e.g., sign, Spanish) to discuss and elaborate on concepts that have been taught in English
42. Carry out lessons on field trips as directed
43. Monitor student performance as directed
44. Reteach or reinforce instructional concepts introduced by teachers to small groups or individual students

Data Collection and Reporting
45. Observe and record student progress in academic areas
46. Observe and record individual student behaviors
47. Observe and record student health needs
48. Observe and record student food and liquid intake
49. Observe and record student bathroom use and needs
50. Observe and record student use of communication skills, adaptive equipment, or devices
51. Observe and record student social interactions, initiative, etc.
52. Observe and record behavior of classes or large or small groups

Activity Preparation and Follow-up
53. Find or arrange materials and equipment (e.g., mix paints, set up lab materials)
54. Adapt materials and equipment as specified for particular student
55. Construct learning materials as directed
56. Construct adapted learning materials according to IEP or other adaptation directions provided by teachers or related service providers
57. Prepare classroom displays
58. Order materials and supplies
59. Organize classroom supplies and materials
60. Operate equipment (e.g., tape recorders, VCRs, overhead projectors)
61. Make audio or visual aids (transparencies, written notes, voice notes, etc.)
62. Schedule guest speakers and visitors as directed
63. Help prepare and clean up after snacks
64. Help students clean up after activities
65. Distribute supplies, materials, and books to students
66. Collect completed work from students and return papers to students
67. Make field trip arrangements (e.g., schedule buses, notify cafeteria)

Ethical Practice
68. Maintain confidentiality of all information regarding students
69. Respect the dignity of every child at all times
70. Report suspected child abuse according to the law, local policies, and procedures
71. Abide by school district policies, school rules, and team standards in all areas
72. Communicate with parents and families only as directed by the teacher
73. Provide accurate and timely information about the student to those who have the right to know (e.g., team members)
74. Carry out all assigned duties responsibly, in a timely manner
75. Protect the welfare and safety of students at all times
76. Maintain composure and emotional control while working with students
77. Demonstrate punctuality and good attendance, and report absences as directed
78. Maintain acceptable hygiene and appearance
79. Protect the privacy and dignity of school staff members, team members, co-workers, other adults in the school
80. Accept assigned tasks graciously
81. Request direction, instruction, or guidance for new or unfamiliar tasks

Table 5.8 continued

Team Participation and Membership
82. Meet with team as scheduled or directed
83. Participate in team meetings by contributing information, ideas, and assistance
84. Participate in team meetings by listening carefully to the ideas of others
85. Engage in appropriate problem-solving steps to resolve problems
86. Engage in mature conflict management steps and processes
87. Use appropriate communication actions in adult-adult interactions
88. Respect the dignity of other adults
89. Participate in learning activities as specified in growth and development plan
90. Participate in schoolwide growth and development activities as specified

Clerical Work
91. Take attendance
92. Type reports, tests, IEPs, assessment reports
93. Make copies
94. Sort and file student papers
95. Record grades
96. Collect fees, i.e., lab, book, milk, activity
97. Correct assigned student lessons or homework
98. Grade tests
99. Help with paperwork to facilitate parent-teacher appointments
100. Inventory materials and fill out routine forms
101. Maintain files for IEPs, assessment reports, other program reports
102. Maintain databases of student information

Health and Personal Related Services
103. Assist students using the restroom
104. Change diapers
105. Clean up after student accidents
106. Help students with health-related services as directed by school nurse (e.g., trach tube suction, nebulizer treatments)
107. Help student(s) eat, mix food, feed (e.g., G-tube)
108. Transfer, turn, position, lift students
109. Assist student to use wheelchair, stander, or other mobility devices
110. Check functioning of assistive equipment (e.g., hearing aid batteries, oxygen tank, tubing)
111. Dispense medication to students according to health plan, as directed by nurse

Other
112. Attend IEP meetings
113. Participate in unit, lesson, and individual student planning sessions with teacher
114. Attend parent-teacher conferences
115. Communication with families (specify _____)
116. Contribute unique skills and talents (specify _____)
117. Attend after-school activities (specify _____)

2. *Ask paraeducator to review list.* The second step is to invite the paraeducator to review the list(s), considering his or her skills, knowledge, and areas of confidence. While it is not necessary to use forms to perform the analysis and comparison, a systematic format, once created, saves time in the future and assures team members that they have addressed all relevant issues. The companion form, the Paraeducator Task Preparation and Confidence Inventory (Table 5.9), may be given to the paraeducator to obtain his or her input.

The lists in Tables 5.8 and 5.9 will need to be adapted to fit the specific characteristics of individual programs and professionals. For example, professionals in a preschool program might eliminate some tasks (e.g., giving spelling tests) and keep others (e.g., self-help, read to students). They might also add tasks that are specific to a program (e.g., work on articulation skills with children). Professionals in a vocational preparation program, on the other hand, might reword a task such as "Help students in drill and practice lessons" to read "Help students apply basic computational skills on the job" to reflect the differences in programmatic emphasis, as well as the age and needs of students. Again, the wide variety of programs, professionals, and student needs precludes the possibility of creating a single list that is entirely useful in all situations. The examples presented are intended as starters from which professionals can create unique lists that address their own program needs.

3. *Analyze the list.* The third step occurs after the list is made and the paraeducator has responded to it. This step is essentially a needs versus preferences analysis in which the professional examines both the master list and the paraeducator's responses to the items to decide which tasks will become an immediate part of the expectations for the paraeducator and which tasks require further preparation.

4. *Create a personalized job description.* The fourth step of defining the job involves creating a personalized job description (PJD). Items on which there is a scoring match (that is, the professional needs the task done and the paraeducator agrees that he or she is prepared to perform it) automatically become part of the PJD. Items for which the need exists, but paraeducator preparation or confidence is lacking, deserve examination and individual evaluation. Some negotiation between the paraeducator and the supervising professional is advisable. The inventories become the vehicle by which these important negotiations are structured. Tasks that the professional needs, but that are not matched by paraeducator training or confidence, may be treated in one of three ways. They may be listed as expected tasks, in which case training must be immediate. They may be listed as future tasks, following appropriate preparation. Or, they may be eliminated from the paraeducator's PJD.

An important caveat here is that the PJD should never exceed the limitations imposed by the official district position description. This is generally not a problem because the items listed in Tables 5.8 and 5.9 are specific examples of the general categories that are typically found on official position descriptions. For example, one category typically found on a paraeducator position description is "Assist with Instruction." Rarely do official position descriptions specify

(text continued on p. 89)

Table 5.9 Paraeducator Task Preparation and Confidence Inventory

Directions for the Paraeducator: *Complete this form by considering your own preparation and confidence to perform each task. Decide how prepared and confident you feel for each task. Circle 1 if you are unprepared to do the task and want or need training in order to begin. Circle 2 to show that you may begin doing the task, but need further instruction. Circle 3 or 4 to show that you want more training to improve your skill. Circle 5 if you feel well prepared and confident.*

Supervision of Groups of Students

1. Assist individual students on arrival or departure (specify _____)   1 2 3 4 5
2. Supervise groups of students during lunch   1 2 3 4 5
3. Supervise groups of students during recess   1 2 3 4 5
4. Supervise groups of students loading and unloading buses   1 2 3 4 5
5. Monitor students during hall passing periods   1 2 3 4 5
6. Escort groups of students to bathroom, library, gym, etc.   1 2 3 4 5
7. Accompany students to therapy sessions, individual appointments, etc.   1 2 3 4 5
8. Teach appropriate social behaviors in common areas   1 2 3 4 5
9. Carry out behavior management   1 2 3 4 5
10. Participate in classroom behavioral system as directed   1 2 3 4 5
11. Provide reinforcement and support in IEPs or behavior plans   1 2 3 4 5
12. Mediate interpersonal conflicts between students   1 2 3 4 5
13. Provide instruction to students on how to mediate their own conflicts   1 2 3 4 5
14. Provide cues or prompts to students who are mediating conflicts   1 2 3 4 5
15. Provide physical proximity for students with behavior problems   1 2 3 4 5
16. Circulate in classroom to provide behavioral supports where needed   1 2 3 4 5
17. Enforce class and school rules   1 2 3 4 5
18. Assist students who are self-managing behavior (e.g., provide cues, prompts)   1 2 3 4 5
19. Help students develop and self-monitor organizational skills   1 2 3 4 5
20. Provide cues or prompts to students to use impulse and anger control strategies   1 2 3 4 5
21. Provide cues or prompts to students to employ specific prosocial skills   1 2 3 4 5
22. Teach prosocial skill lessons   1 2 3 4 5
23. Facilitate appropriate social interactions among students   1 2 3 4 5
24. Assist other students in coping with the behaviors of specific students   1 2 3 4 5

Delivery of Instruction

25. Conduct drill and practice activities (e.g., vocabulary, math facts, articulation protocols)   1 2 3 4 5
26. Read or repeat tests or directions to students   1 2 3 4 5

Table 5.9   continued

27.	Read with students (specify techniques _____ [e.g., guided oral reading, neurological impress, repeated readings, choral reading])	1 2 3 4 5
28.	Help students complete written assignments	1 2 3 4 5
29.	Give objective tests (e.g., spelling, math)	1 2 3 4 5
30.	Assist students to compose original work (e.g., stories, essays, reports)	1 2 3 4 5
31.	Tape-record stories, lessons, assignments	1 2 3 4 5
32.	Create individualized instructional materials according to the adaptation list provided or specific directions (e.g., lesson plans, IEPs)	1 2 3 4 5
33.	Read to students (specify _____ [e.g., text material, stories])	1 2 3 4 5
34.	Listen to students reading orally	1 2 3 4 5
35.	Help students work on individual projects	1 2 3 4 5
36.	Facilitate students' active participation in cooperative groups	1 2 3 4 5
37.	Help students select library books and reference materials	1 2 3 4 5
38.	Help students use computers (specify purpose [e.g., keyboarding, drill and practice, composing written assignments, printing, Internet)	1 2 3 4 5
39.	Translate instruction or student responses (e.g., sign or other language)	1 2 3 4 5
40.	Translate directions into other language for student(s) (e.g., ASL)	1 2 3 4 5
41.	Translate teacher-made materials or text materials into another language	1 2 3 4 5
42.	Use another language (e.g., sign, Spanish), to discuss and elaborate on concepts that have been taught in English	1 2 3 4 5
43.	Carry out lessons on field trips as directed	1 2 3 4 5
44.	Monitor student performance as directed	1 2 3 4 5
45.	Reteach or reinforce instructional concepts introduced by teachers to small groups or individual students	1 2 3 4 5

Data Collection and Reporting

46.	Observe and record student progress in academic areas	1 2 3 4 5
47.	Observe and record individual student behaviors	1 2 3 4 5
48.	Observe and record student health needs	1 2 3 4 5
49.	Observe and record student food and liquid intake	1 2 3 4 5
50.	Observe and record student bathroom use and needs	1 2 3 4 5
51.	Observe and record student communication skills, adaptive equipment	1 2 3 4 5
52.	Observe and record student social interactions, initiative, etc.	1 2 3 4 5
53.	Observe and record behavior of classes or large or small groups	1 2 3 4 5

Activity Preparation and Follow-up

54.	Find or arrange materials and equipment (e.g., mix paints, set up lab materials)	1 2 3 4 5

Table 5.9 continued

55.	Adapt materials and equipment as specified for particular student	1	2	3	4	5
56.	Construct learning materials as directed	1	2	3	4	5
57.	Prepare classroom displays	1	2	3	4	5
58.	Order materials and supplies	1	2	3	4	5
59.	Organize classroom supplies or materials	1	2	3	4	5
60.	Operate equipment (e.g., tape recorders, VCRs, overhead projectors)	1	2	3	4	5
61.	Make audio or visual aids (transparencies, written notes, voice notes, etc.)	1	2	3	4	5
62.	Schedule guest speakers and visitors as directed	1	2	3	4	5
63.	Help prepare and clean up after snacks	1	2	3	4	5
64.	Help students clean up after activities	1	2	3	4	5
65.	Distribute supplies, materials, and books to students	1	2	3	4	5
66.	Collect completed work from students and return papers to students	1	2	3	4	5
67.	Make field trip arrangements (e.g., schedule buses, notify cafeteria)	1	2	3	4	5

Ethical Practice

68.	Maintain confidentiality of all information regarding students	1	2	3	4	5
69.	Respect the dignity of every child at all times	1	2	3	4	5
70.	Report suspected child abuse according to the law, local policies, procedures	1	2	3	4	5
71.	Abide by school district policies, school rules, and team standards in all areas	1	2	3	4	5
72.	Communicate with parents and families only as directed by the teacher	1	2	3	4	5
73.	Provide accurate and timely information about the student to those who have the right and the need to know (e.g., team members)	1	2	3	4	5
74.	Carry out all assigned duties responsibly, in a timely manner	1	2	3	4	5
75.	Protect the welfare and safety of students at all times	1	2	3	4	5
76.	Maintain composure and emotional control while working with students	1	2	3	4	5
77.	Demonstrate punctuality and good attendance, and report absences as directed	1	2	3	4	5
78.	Maintain acceptable hygiene and appearance	1	2	3	4	5
79.	Protect the privacy and dignity of school staff members, team members, co-workers, and other adults in the school	1	2	3	4	5
80.	Accept assigned tasks graciously	1	2	3	4	5
81.	Request direction, instruction, or guidance for new or unfamiliar tasks	1	2	3	4	5

Team Participation and Membership

82.	Meet with team as scheduled or directed	1	2	3	4	5
83.	Participate in team meetings by contributing information, ideas, and assistance	1	2	3	4	5
84.	Participate in team meetings by listening carefully to the ideas of others	1	2	3	4	5
85.	Engage in appropriate problem-solving steps to resolve problems	1	2	3	4	5
86.	Engage in mature conflict management steps and processes	1	2	3	4	5

Table 5.9 continued

87.	Use appropriate communication actions in adult-adult interactions	1	2	3	4	5
88.	Respect the dignity of other adults	1	2	3	4	5
89.	Participate in learning activities as specified in growth and development plan	1	2	3	4	5
90.	Participate in schoolwide growth and development activities as specified	1	2	3	4	5

Clerical Work

91.	Take attendance	1	2	3	4	5
92.	Type reports, tests, IEPs, assessment reports	1	2	3	4	5
93.	Make copies	1	2	3	4	5
94.	Sort and file student papers	1	2	3	4	5
95.	Record grades	1	2	3	4	5
96.	Collect fees, i.e., lab, book, milk, activity	1	2	3	4	5
97.	Correct assigned student lessons or homework	1	2	3	4	5
98.	Grade tests	1	2	3	4	5
99.	Help with paperwork to facilitate parent-teacher appointments	1	2	3	4	5
100.	Inventory materials and fill out routine forms					
101.	Maintain files for IEPs, assessment reports, other program reports	1	2	3	4	5
102.	Maintain databases of student information	1	2	3	4	5

Health and Personal Related Services

103.	Assist students using the restroom	1	2	3	4	5
104.	Change diapers	1	2	3	4	5
105.	Clean up after student accidents	1	2	3	4	5
106.	Help students with health-related services as directed by school nurse (e.g., trach tube suction, nebulizer treatments)	1	2	3	4	5
107.	Help student(s) eat, mix food, feed (e.g., G-tube)	1	2	3	4	5
108.	Transfer, turn, position, lift students	1	2	3	4	5
109.	Assist student to use wheelchair, stander, or other mobility devices	1	2	3	4	5
110.	Check functioning of equipment (e.g., hearing aid batteries, oxygen tank)	1	2	3	4	5
111.	Dispense medication to students according to health plan, as directed by nurse	1	2	3	4	5

Other

112.	Attend IEP meetings	1	2	3	4	5
113.	Participate in unit, lesson, and individual student planning sessions with teacher	1	2	3	4	5
114.	Attend parent-teacher conferences	1	2	3	4	5
115.	Communication with families (specify _____)	1	2	3	4	5
116.	Contribute unique skills and talents (specify _____)	1	2	3	4	5
117.	Attend after-school activities (specify _____)	1	2	3	4	5

Table 5.10   Training List Matrix

Task for Which Skills Are Needed[a]	Name the Skill or Competency[b]	Who Could Possibly Provide Training[c]	When Might the Training Occur[d]
1.			
2.			
3.			
4.			
5.			
6.			
7.			
8.			
9.			
10.			

a. Describe the duty to be performed (e.g., playground supervision).
b. Note the competency required of the paraeducator to be successful at performing the task (e.g., for playground supervision, mediating conflicts between students is a competency).
c. Indicate (either by name or by position title) who could or might be able to provide training. Don't forget to consider other paraeducators, students, teachers, related service providers, administrators, etc.
d. Identify a possible timeframe. Stating a particular date doesn't create a binding contract by any means, but sets an expectation. It also provides a sense of when the supervisor can realistically expect the paraeducator to begin performing the duty as expected.

what such assistance is composed of. The PJD gives definition to the category by describing the specific actions to be taken by the paraeducator.

5. *Determine training needs.* The fifth and final step of job definition involves creating a list of tasks for which the paraeducator requires training to develop the skills or competencies he or she will need. The matrix shown in Table 5.10 can be used to list the tasks for which training is needed, as well as ideas about when the training might occur and who might provide it.

Keep the Momentum

The third stage of orientation occurs anytime after the first week of a paraeducator's employment, but within the first month. There are only two steps in this phase, and both involve fine-tuning the supervisory relationship. First, a review of the training plan developed during the second stage of orientation is useful. There may be areas of skill development that arise after the initial conversation that should be added to the list at this point. Second, it is wise to review a list of all personnel at this point to make sure that the paraeducator has met everyone involved in the building and with students. By the end of the first month of employment, a paraeducator should be able to easily make a distinction between who is a school employee and who is not. The third stage of orientation establishes a cycle that is continued through ongoing training. Systematic, ongoing training will be discussed in Chapter 8 and performance feedback will be covered in Chapter 9.

CHAPTER SUMMARY

All new employees deserve basic orientation to the job. The first stage of orientation should include introductions to the closest coworkers, workplace policies, safety and discipline procedures, and issues of confidentiality. The second stage of orientation establishes the supervisory relationship. It includes introductions to other coworkers and school staff that the paraeducator will work with less frequently. Then a structured get-to-know-you conversation follows. Analyses of personal work style preferences and a discussion of how differences will be handled should follow soon after. Finally, a personalized job description should be created that specifies which tasks the paraeducator will be expected to perform and identify at the same time those tasks for which further training is necessary. The third stage of orientation creates a momentum for further training and ongoing supervision.

6 Taking Time to Save Time: Delegating to Paraeducators

As Steve was walking out to his car one evening, he reviewed his day. He hadn't had time to think all day. He mused, "Going to work is like stepping into a boxing ring: I walk in the door and get hit. Just about the time I rebound from the ropes, I get hit again. I go home too exhausted to organize or think about the next day, and, over time, I feel myself becoming less and less effective." Steve isn't so different from thousands of other school professionals. He reacts to the demands of the situation, without feeling like he's really on top of them or even in charge of them. Some days, he doesn't get any of the things on his "to do" list done.

As he walks out to the parking lot, he notices that his is the only car there. "Always the last car in the lot," he mutters. When he gets home, his little daughter says, "Daddy, look at my dolls, they're giving a play!" He answers, "Sorry, honey. I have some work to do." "Daddy," she says, "why do you always have homework?" Sadly, he answers, "I just don't have time to get it done at school." She wanders down the hall, then turns and says, "Daddy, maybe the teacher should put you in a slower group."

Steve doesn't need a "slower group"; he needs to learn to delegate. If you've ever felt like your day was spent in a boxing ring, you may need to acquire some delegation awareness, too.

WHAT IS DELEGATION?

Delegation is a process of getting things done through others who have the competence to handle them. It is also a process for helping people become as good as they can be and maybe even better than they dreamed. It's a one-way ticket to success for your school, your program, and your students. When you delegate to a paraeducator you give that person the authority to get tasks done without giving up your responsibility for your school, your program, or your students. Maintaining responsibility while delegating is the key to your effectiveness as a school professional. This means that you must take time up front to save time in the end while increasing your effectiveness in the long run.

Delegation, done well, is an art. It is the art of achieving specific predefined results through empowerment and motivation of others. *Predefined* means advanced thinking about what you're trying to accomplish in your school, in your program, or with your students. *Empowerment* means making paraeducators feel powerful over some aspects of their jobs. You can think of it as *sharing* power with paraeducators. It involves motivating paraeducators to do their best. The art of delegating is developed over time. When we first start teaching, we spend a lot of time *doing* to master our craft and our art. As we become more skilled, we are better equipped to *direct* rather than *do*. If, over the years, we remain overinvolved in doing, we have failed to grow in our art and craft.

What Delegation Is Not

Too often, school professionals have experienced bad practices that were mislabeled "delegation." For this reason, it is important to distinguish what delegation is not from the description of delegation.

Dumping. Dumping is a practice that minimizes the paraeducator role. It shows genuine disrespect for the paraeducator because it involves dumping tasks that are so trivial that the paraeducator never experiences genuine accomplishment. Moreover, dumping ignores the match between tasks and paraeducator abilities. An example of dumping is when, at the last minute, the professional asks the paraeducator to run an errand, copy a worksheet, or find materials that should have been found earlier. It suggests that the professional is unorganized and fundamentally unprepared to supervise the paraeducator.

Puppeteering. Puppeteering means that the supervisor either fails to give the authority to make the decisions involved in carrying out the tasks or micromanages the task once it's been delegated to the paraeducator. Sometimes puppeteering takes the form of providing too much detail to the paraeducator, but sometimes it shows up as meddling. Either way, puppeteering is a lose-lose proposition.

Passing the Buck. Passing the buck usually occurs when there has been a failure in accomplishments and the supervisor blames the paraeducator for that failure. Effective delegation does not include passing the buck. When failures happen, the effective school professional admits responsibility and takes positive steps to correct the problems.

Punishment. Punishment does not motivate paraeducators to give their best. When a supervisor mean-spiritedly assigns much more than a person can conceivably do, or when tasks are assigned in ways that are demeaning or trivial, they may have the effect of diminishing initiative and ownership by punishing the paraeducator. Punishment tends to make people angry and defensive. They feel powerless and demeaned. It breaks down whatever trust has been established.

Why Should I Delegate to Paraeducators?

There are 10 reasons to delegate.

1. Delegation Makes the Most of Your Time

Effective delegation means that you are making the most of your time. Admittedly, it takes time to delegate, to motivate paraeducators to do their jobs correctly, to communicate well, to organize instructional and managerial tasks, and to plan and prepare for paraeducators. However, by delegating some tasks to paraeducators, you accomplish more work on behalf of more students, in the same number of hours.

2. Delegation Creates Teams

Teams get more work done than individuals do, in the same amount of time. By delegating to paraeducators, you create a sense of shared commitment to the needs of your students, your classroom, your program, and your school. You also establish a bond in which members cover for one another in difficult moments. They step up and take initiative for the work that needs to be done. They offer ideas and suggestions aimed to improve the overall goals of the group. Delegating important work to paraeducators imparts a sense of respect for who they are and what they do. Your respect motivates them to contribute even more to the team effort.

3. Delegation Empowers Paraeducators

When you teach a paraeducator to do the work of instructing students, assisting students with their health and social needs, supervising students, and monitoring students in common areas, you give them dignity, respect, and power. Sure, there is the possibility that an eager beaver will go on to become a teacher, eventually replacing you, but in the meantime, it gives you the chance to move on to learn and do new and more exciting, interesting things. If you have a paraeducator you consider an eager beaver, you won't be able to stop him or her anyhow, so why not help the paraeducator learn all he or she can? Meanwhile, constantly improve and renew yourself. Teachers and administrators who have old skills, in spite of lots of longevity, are not particularly respected in schools and have few opportunities to do new and interesting things. School professionals who continually grow and improve their skills have great luck at getting more interesting and challenging assignments. Luck happens at the intersection of preparation and opportunity.

4. Delegation Means You Don't Have to Do Everything Yourself

You don't want to do it all yourself, do you? The boxing ring analogy Steve thought about was apt because he was stuck in thinking that he had to do it all himself. As he tried to react and respond to every crisis or request in his day, it reinforced his need to be needed, but did little to improve his ability to actually be effective. If you are willing to take a look at your need to be needed and give that up to improve your effectiveness, delegation is the mechanism by which to accomplish it.

5. *Delegation Maximizes Use of Your Personal Resources*

Your strength, energy, creativity, and knowledge are taxed unfairly when you have to use them to cover every base, respond to every emergency, figure out every detail, manage every behavior problem, initiate every parent contact, and do all the instruction. There is no reason to waste your talents this way. When you delegate to others, you reserve some of your energy and strength to do the things that are most important for you to do, while making sure that everything else gets done, too.

6. *Delegation Gives Paraeducators What They Need*

Paraeducators want to be told what to do—to be given direction. Some school professionals, particularly those who are good problem solvers and are very self-directed, fail to realize that paraeducators want direction. Often, paraeducators don't want the job of a teacher. Often they want to leave school at the end of the day and go about their lives doing other things, without the responsibilities of teachers. It's their choice—they are sustainers, they do important work with students, they do it effectively, they get it done, they are good solid workers and team players, but they are not teachers. They want, need, and deserve direction.

7. *Delegation Challenges Paraeducators*

Challenging tasks and assignments mean that paraeducators stretch themselves and their skills. They achieve more. You recognize them for their efforts and the results of their work, and their esteem goes up. As their esteem increases, they become more motivated to do the work well. They come to believe that they can take on new challenges successfully. Delegating meaningful and significant work to paraeducators provides that challenge and results in higher achievement for students.

8. *Delegation Avoids the Creation of Indispensable People*

Some school professionals make themselves indispensable by making sure that no one else can do any of the work they do. On the other hand, a more effective professional makes sure that paraeducators can do some of the work, so when the professional has too much to do all at once, or when the professional must be away from the building for a day, the work continues. Students gain consistency and feel secure. In addition, delegation to multiple paraeducators, where there are several in a school, means that one absence doesn't create havoc in the school or program. And it ensures that when one moves or leaves the position, others can step up to the plate.

9. *Delegation Gives Schools a Better Return on Personnel Dollars*

Teachers, psychologists, occupational therapists, nurses, and librarians are relatively expensive in a school budget. It makes sense that every school professional would want to make sure that the right task is being performed or accomplished at the most cost-effective level. Delegation helps limited budgets stretch as far as possible. Delegation pushes the task down in the organizational structure to the place where the accomplishment of it will present the greatest challenge, but where it will successfully be accomplished. Successful businesses run on these principles. So do effective schools.

10. Delegation Minimizes Physical Limitations

Laborers work from the neck down; that is, their bodies perform the work for which they are paid. They are limited in the work they can do by the physical limitations imposed by certain external variables such as time, location, and space. When performing physical labor, a person cannot be in two places at once, cannot work in multiple locations, and cannot move from one place to another instantly. School professionals, on the other hand, work mostly from the neck up. They use knowledge, skills, and judgment to direct the work of educating students, rather than trying to be everywhere at once, running from place to place, and racing to meet one need after another. By working from the neck up, professionals have fewer limitations as to what they can accomplish. It is an example of working smarter, not harder—a notion first introduced in Chapter 3. Delegation is the answer to working from the neck up and minimizing the physical limitations of time, location, and space.

Why Do We Fail to Delegate?

Take a moment to ask yourself why you have failed to delegate when you could have? First, jot your thoughts down and then compare them to the reasons listed below. Once you understand your own reasons, you can begin to think about how you can use your time more wisely through delegation. But, be kind to yourself. Few school professionals were prepared to supervise other adults. You may have never thought of yourself as a manager of other adults. You probably began your career believing that you, and you alone, would have to do it all. You are not alone. For years, other school professionals, like you, have had little preparation to manage a schedule that includes collaborative planning, coteaching, and supervision of paraeducators.

There are also 10 reasons why school professionals fail to delegate.

1. Paraeducators Are Paid Too Little and Work Too Hard for Their Pay

Sometimes teachers perceive that paraeducators are overworked for what they're paid. While it's true that paraeducators are not well paid, this perception may or may not be valid. It's worth checking on how paraeducators are using their time. Remember, presence and productivity are not synonymous. Activity and productivity are not synonymous. In fact, paraeducators may be doing unproductive tasks if you haven't provided the best direction, training, coaching, or monitoring possible.

Moreover, a paraeducator position is a real position. It isn't a highly paid position, but it is real and important. Not all tasks are fun and some are less pleasant than others. If a person worked at McDonald's and was assigned the tasks of mopping the bathroom floors at the end of every shift, that person would be required to do that task, even though he or she is paid poorly. Low pay is an insufficient reason to fail to give paraeducators work that needs to be done.

2. I Am a Perfectionist and I Want to Be Sure It Gets Done Right

Only one person can do the job exactly as you would—you. If you make the choice to delegate to paraeducators, you will no longer perform every task. To cope with this mental shift, you must ask yourself this fundamental question, and you will probably have to memorize it and ask it of yourself over and over again: "Does this task need to be done to a level of perfection?"

We pay an enormous premium for perfection wherever we decide to achieve it—it costs almost as much time and money to go the last 10% to get it "just right" as it takes to go the first 90% of the trip. So, to ask whether a task warrants being done perfectly allows you to place your resources—time, energy, and money—in the right places. The second question to ask is, "Can someone else do the task to an acceptable level?" If the answer is positive, we assign those things that don't need to be done perfectly to paraeducators.

3. I Have No Time to Train Paraeducators

This is a barrier if you are overbooked already. In most schools, conscientious professionals are doing a workload and a half. There isn't enough time at the moment to provide the training to others to do the job. The self-commitment to delegate, however, holds the promise that time spent training paraeducators pays off in the long run by freeing you of some of the tasks you were so busy doing. Initially, however, something gets left undone. Training does take time and the time has to be taken from some other task.

4. Teaching Is for Teachers and Speech-Language Therapy Is for Therapists

This expectation, that you have to do all the teaching or service delivery personally, derives from some misguided professional standards that would suggest that there are no parts of your job—no aspects of instruction or therapy—that can be done by another person. This is simply untrue. While the important aspects of instructional planning and decision making require the judgment and professional knowledge gained through preparation programs and experience, many aspects of instruction are routine. Listening to students practice oral reading, encouraging students to remain on task while doing assignments, monitoring students as they take tests, helping students locate reference or reading materials, and assisting students as they set up lab equipment are all tasks that are part of instruction and can be performed by paraeducators.

5. A Paraeducator Isn't Qualified to Do the Job

Even with training, some people are innately unqualified to do the work. Not everyone can be a paraeducator. It takes certain qualities, dispositions, and skills to provide instructional support. If we delegate to a person who does not have the personal qualities, dispositions, or skills, we do an injustice to our students. The only other consideration here is whether the individual paraeducator can be coached, taught, or disciplined to display the qualities, dispositions, or skills needed to perform the work. If not, administrators, teachers, and other professionals must work together to document the paraeducator's lack of necessary job-related equipment.

6. *Some Parts of Teaching Are My Occupational Hobby*

You like doing some things, even though they aren't the most important parts of your work—watching students practice a play, making bulletin boards, monitoring the playground, or grading spelling tests. These tasks are hard to let go, but if they are keeping you from doing important thinking about student assessment and students' needs, instructional or curricular planning and design, determining programmatic goals, and adapting to the unique needs of individual students, then these tasks are minimizing your effectiveness. You are neglecting the things that are most important in exchange for the momentary pleasure of doing the things that you think are fun. Consider what you bring to your students. You bring curricular and instructional knowledge. You know how to assess student achievement and progress. You know the kinds of questions learners ask when they are just beginning to understand the subject. This knowledge is wasted if you spend too much time doing routine tasks and too little time assessing and diagnosing their learning needs and planning the curriculum and instruction for them. You may be cheating your students out of the best you have to offer.

7. *It's Not Part of the Paraeducator's Job Description*

While there are legal limits imposed by the official district job description for a paraeducator, most job descriptions are vague. They tend to offer only the general categories of tasks that paraeducators may perform. It is relatively easy to add tasks and assignments as long as they don't go beyond the categories listed. Remember that the personalized job description process, as described in Chapter 5, allows items to be added as current expectations pending immediate training and as future expectations after training is completed. If we limit paraeducators to what they can safely and comfortably do now, we encourage their stagnation and fail to help them expand their abilities to perform the work we need them to do.

8. *I'm Not Confident of the Paraeducator's Work*

This tends to be the reason for lack of delegation if there is a history of past failures or if past performance just didn't measure up. You can continue to fail to delegate for this reason, unless you want to improve your own effectiveness. In that case, you must first recognize that you never forgave the paraeducator for the first mistake or poor performance. You have to decide to forgive before you can allow yourself to delegate a similar task again. Immediately after forgiveness, however, you have to provide instruction and direction on how you want the task performed, what the outcomes and expectations are, and how you will monitor the completion of the task. You must consider how the paraeducator's previous failures or poor performance may have been related to your lack of appropriate supervision.

9. *I Can Do It Faster Myself*

This may be a valid reason not to delegate a task to someone else. If it takes ten minutes to delegate the task and you could do it in two minutes, why would you want to make that eight-minute time investment? It depends. If the deadline is rapidly approaching and you cannot possibly spare eight minutes, you wouldn't. On the other hand, if the paraeducator needs to do this type of activity to gain skill, get recognition, enhance his or her career development, or do something that's fun and enjoyable, you may want to take the time. Or, when the task is recurring, and you will have to do it again and again, it provides cumulative timesavings to teach the paraeducator to do it.

10. *I Don't Want to Be Bossy—I Want Paraeducators to Like Me*

Many of us were raised by parents who told us not to act bossy or to tell others what to do. Mothers warn children that no one will like them if they are bossy. Yet, when the role of "boss" seems legitimate, we are easily able to overcome mother's warning. With our students, we give direction, correct inappropriate or unacceptable behavior, provide corrective feedback, and teach new skills. Yet, with paraeducators (probably because they are adults) we revert to the message mother gave us—don't act bossy!

Delegation awareness must include the understanding of the legitimate role of teacher, related service provider, or administrator as boss. Being the boss is not a bad thing and in every business there are people who supervise others and provide direction to their work. People don't automatically dislike their bosses. They only dislike them when they use poor interpersonal skills, have negative attitudes, fail to give the necessary authority to do the work, or fail to provide adequate instruction and direction, or when they unfairly blame the worker for failing on an assignment.

When we fail to delegate effectively there are two potentially disastrous results. The first is that we inadvertently lock in low performers and force out high performers. Low performers tend to stay. If no one pushes the envelope, a poor performer stays on, giving little, yet getting a paycheck. No one increases expectations, teaches new skills, or monitors performance. Failure to delegate costs the school district enormous amounts of money. People are being paid to do little—to be unproductive and ineffective. Students suffer from lack of other resources that might have been purchased with the wasted dollars.

At the same time, high performers aren't challenged if delegation is poor. They do only the minimal tasks because no one provides the incentive or the training to do more, learn more, or take on new assignments. Eventually, high performers suffer stagnation and leave. The school and district lose a potentially great employee and students lose the benefit of a talented paraeducator.

A second potential disaster is that, over time, the position begins to attract low performers. Word gets out in the community. Because paraeducators typically come from the local community, you can be sure that the proverbial grapevine is alive and well. If the grapevine has it that the job is easy, doesn't require much, and doesn't expect much, you will attract applicants who are potentially poor performers. On other hand, when we expect a lot, give appropriate direction, feedback, and respect, we attract the best applicants for open positions.

What Can I Delegate to a Paraeducator?

Delegation frees the school professional to do the work that cannot be delegated—such as assessing students; designing materials; planning curriculum, instruction, therapy, and adaptations; coteaching with other teachers; and consulting with other professionals. It increases your productivity because you double the amount of work that gets done. Responsible delegation emphasizes that you continue to manage instruction for your students, without having to do everything yourself. Box 3.2 describes the major categories of tasks that may be delegated to paraeducators and Table 5.6 provides specific details about the types of tasks that are perfectly acceptable to delegate. Of course, personal preferences and skills must be considered in the delegation process, but the tools to assess those preferences and skills have already been described in Chapter 5.

In addition, consider delegating tasks of a recurring nature. If you have to do it every day, every week, or every month, it is recurring and may be something that could be done by a paraeducator. For example, do you have to submit reports on Medicaid billable services provided to students with significant health support needs? Perhaps the paraeducator could assemble that information for you each month.

Also remember that some minor decisions can be made by paraeducators. If you provide the guidelines on the types of adaptations that are always appropriate for a particular student with unique needs, a paraeducator is very capable of making decisions within the guidelines about how to dress up the materials or what variations on the adaptation to use at a particular moment.

Consider, too, the skills and talents of the individual paraeducator. Sometimes you have the good fortune to work with a person who has skills that complement rather than duplicate yours. Give a task to the paraeducator who is better qualified to do it and you create time to do the assessment, planning, and instructional decision making that you are uniquely qualified to do.

When Do I Have Time to Delegate to Paraeducators?

Delegation requires effective time management. To manage your time well, you need to consider every task in terms of two factors: its urgency and its importance. A task is urgent if you are being pushed to attend to it or to complete it immediately. It may be your policy to avoid interrupting your instructional time, but if an upset parent comes to your door, you will probably make an exception and respond to the urgency of the situation. However, not every interruption is worth responding to. Some interruptions only have the appearance of urgency. Every knock at the door has the appearance of urgency. Only when the person enters and begins telling you what they came for can you assess whether the issue is really so important that it couldn't have been dealt with at a later time, along with other issues. It is quite reasonable to ask interrupters to make an appointment to meet with you later or to schedule a regular meeting time during which you can handle all the issues they have saved up.

Of course, this fills your schedule with meetings, but it puts you in control of your work rather than letting your work control you.

Of course, there are always differences in perceptions as to whether an item is important enough to merit immediate attention. You may need to discuss the issue at the moment of interruption, but you can also ask the interrupter's perspective on the importance and urgency of the issue, explain your view of priorities, share your rationale for saving up various topics of conversation for a common meeting time, and ask the interrupter to jot a list of concerns so you can be sure to attend to all of them.

The second factor, importance, is measured by how much the task contributes to your overall purposes, outcomes for students, or program goals. You decide whether the importance of a task means that you have to do it yourself or whether you can delegate it to someone and get the result you need.

Considering those two factors, tasks may be placed into one of four quadrants on the Delegation Decision Matrix (Table 6.1). Notice that the tasks located in the upper right quadrant (Quadrant II), for the most part, are tasks you probably want to "Do" yourself. Tasks in the Do quadrant are not appropriately delegated to a paraeducator. You may find that these tasks are difficult to get to because they are not so urgent—unless you ignore them long enough. Yet, each of these tasks carries major importance to your overall effectiveness as a school professional. Deferring and delegating these tasks are bad choices if you want to be effective. Although school professionals may also choose to do the tasks that fall into the upper left quadrant (Quadrant I) themselves, many of them are appropriate for delegation to a paraeducator. School professionals who delegate tasks appropriately take these factors into account along with the skills, preferences, program needs, and personalized job description of the paraeducator.

The lower left quadrant (Quadrant III) contains tasks that are appropriately delegated to a paraeducator, but may also be deferred until more pressing issues are completed. You may want to keep two in-baskets or two to-do lists for the paraeducator, labeled "Deadlines" and "No Deadlines." A paraeducator first finishes the tasks in the deadlines basket, but when unexpected downtimes occur, or when he or she has a free moment, tasks from the No Deadline basket can be addressed.

Quadrant IV only includes tasks that do not result in consequences of major significance. The tasks are also not pressing. Quadrant IV tasks may be delegated to a paraeducator, but for the most part, they are tasks that should simply be discarded—not done by anyone. The key words for the lower right quadrant are "Defer" and "Discard."

The Seven-Step Delegation Method

Delegation consists of a series of seven steps. You may want to memorize and follow these steps as you delegate to paraeducators. Some tasks are quite simple and require little thought or preparation to delegate. Others are more complex, and all of the steps deserve attention. The most complex tasks deserve to have written directions.

Table 6.1 Delegation Decision Matrix for School Professionals

	High Urgency	Low Urgency
High Importance	✓ Student behavior crises ✓ Meetings re: crises ✓ Student health crises ✓ Monitoring students in nonclassroom settings ✓ Certain documentation and paperwork ✓ Taking attendance and lunch counts ✓ Implementing behavior plans, health plans, curricular modifications, and adaptations during student contact hours Key "D" Words: Do Now / Delegate Now	✓ Assessment of students' progress ✓ Designing individual behavior, health plans, and curricular adaptations ✓ Assessment of students for program eligibility ✓ Long-range planning of instruction and lesson planning ✓ Curriculum development and planning ✓ Building relationships among professionals and working collaboratively ✓ Coplanning interventions, curriculum, and instruction ✓ Meeting to provide supervision to paraeducators ✓ Assessment of student progress and program eligibility ✓ Conferring with other professionals ✓ Meeting to direct the work of paraeducators ✓ Meeting to provide supervision to paraeducators ✓ Conferring with parents and families ✓ Organizing office space, files, materials for quick retrieval Key "D" Word: Do Soon
Low Importance	✓ General office announcements ✓ Selected mail, fliers ✓ Selected meetings ✓ Certain interruptions ✓ Some unscheduled parent visits ✓ Grading some daily student work Key "D" Words: Delegate / Defer	✓ Selected copy work, filing ✓ Selected mail ✓ Selected phone calls ✓ Selected teachers' lounge conversations ✓ Selected classroom decorating activities ✓ Selected record keeping, filing, and cleaning up Key "D" Words: Defer /Discard

SOURCE: Adapted from French (1997).

1. *Set clear objectives.* Many teachers provide paraeducators with the details of what they want done. They name the activity and the materials, but sometimes forget to point out what the intended outcome is. As a result, paraeducators may inadvertently make mistakes. Barbara, a paraeducator at McKinley, worked with Eric, a fifth-grade student with Down Syndrome who also has low muscle tone and respiratory care needs. Several professionals have contributed to Eric's IEP, so various professionals give directions to Barbara on how to work

with Eric. One day, Barbara had Eric and a small group of his fifth-grade friends engaged in an activity with soap bubbles blown from a little wand. The kids were having a great time, reaching and bursting the bubbles as they floated toward the ground, then stepping on the ones that neared the ground. Eric was laughing and enjoying himself, clearly part of the group and having a wonderful time. The university professor, visiting her student teachers that day, happened to stop at the door of the special education room while this activity was in full swing. She noted the mutual enjoyment all the students were getting from the activity, but she wondered about the purpose of the activity because Eric had so few opportunities to reach for or actually touch any of the bubbles. Obviously, his typical peers were adept at this, but he was not. Their eagerness and natural abilities overshadowed his ability to participate. Yet, he was enjoying himself. When the activity was over, she stepped in beside Barbara on the way back toward the classroom. She asked Barbara about the purpose of the activity and Barbara admitted that she didn't know about any purpose. She had been told what to do, but had never been told why. The professor pursued an answer to her question. She guessed, correctly it turned out, that the purpose of the activity was for Eric to improve his coordination. And she realized that Barbara had inadvertently failed to give Eric the experiences he needed by failing to impose restrictions on the other students. Barbara made a simple adjustment, once she understood the purpose of the activity, which required the typical peers to count slowly to 10 before they were allowed to reach for a bubble, giving Eric time to respond. Barbara had misdirected a seemingly simple activity because no one told her the purpose of the activity and she was able to do it more effectively once she knew the intended outcomes.

2. *Select the right person.* If more than one paraeducator or other human resources are available (e.g., volunteers, peer tutors, peer coaches), you have a choice. At Rampart High School, a schoolwide peer support program prepares typical students to assist special education students. Sometimes the typical peer may take notes for another student or may redirect a student who has difficulty attending to tasks. Sometimes peers help classmates regain composure during stressful moments. The special education teacher, Mr. Wright, makes decisions regarding whether he will delegate a particular task to a peer or to a paraeducator. A situation that developed in the vocal music class is an example. Laura, a special education student, had become infatuated with one of her classmates and insisted on standing next to him in the choir. Ms. Myers, the vocal music teacher, had her hands full with the 105 students in her choir and requested help from the special education team. Mr. Wright came to the choir room to assess the situation. Once he understood the problem Laura was having, he decided that he should assign a paraeducator to the situation on a temporary basis (three weeks) rather than try to employ the services of a peer. He had to instruct the paraeducator how she should help the student stay in her place and attend to the teacher. He also specifically told her how to begin to fade her help as soon as Laura began to do what she was asked.

The corollary to selecting the right person is using the skills or talents one person has to that person's best advantage. If a paraeducator is particularly skillful in a particular area, it may make sense to delegate those tasks to him or her regularly. For example, Ivory, an experienced paraeducator, is a particularly gifted storyteller. The school professionals with whom she works all recognize and value her accomplishments in story telling. They frequently find opportunities to take advantage of this unique contribution that Ivory makes to their school.

On the other hand, paraeducators grow and develop as they are assigned challenging work and they learn to do it. Edee was reluctant at first to use the computer in the special education program, but when the team urged her to gradually take on some computer-based record keeping, she found that her fear of the technology dissipated as her skills grew.

You may also recognize that some tasks are more unpleasant than others. Even if a person is very good at an unpleasant duty, that duty should be rotated and shared by others. For example, diaper changing is sometimes necessary. It is a task that no one really likes to do. Yet, it is important and oftentimes sensitive. It also has a tremendous impact on the student. The student's privacy is at stake and his or her dignity must be preserved during such an intimate procedure. You will want to ensure student privacy and dignity while fairly rotating unpleasant tasks. Suzanna, a third-grade teacher at Thatcher Elementary School, works with Lane, a paraeducator assigned to her classroom. Lane is assigned to the third-grade classroom on behalf of Melinda, a child with significant support needs. Melinda needs *freshening* (as they like to call it) every few hours. Sometimes Suzanna takes Melinda to the *private corner* to do the freshening while Lane continues working with students on math skills. At most other times, Lane takes Melinda while Suzanna continues with the class. Neither one likes diaper changing but Suzanna understands the fairness of sharing the task.

3. *Train the paraeducator to carry out the tasks.* Anytime you delegate a task that a paraeducator has not performed before, you have to go through a quick mental checklist, considering what you already know about his or her skills and confidence on various tasks and then providing training on tasks that are new, that have new variations, or for which the paraeducator had little skill or confidence. Or, consider who else might be able to train the paraeducator to do the task. It may be a better use of your time to ask another paraeducator to teach a skill, demonstrate a technique, or explain a procedure than it is for you to do it. You want to be sure that she knows how to do all or part of what you're delegating, whether you do it or someone else does. Over time, in a well-established working relationship, you'll know the paraeducator's skills and the training effect will be cumulative, but until then, plan time for training sessions for every new task.

4. *Get input from the paraeducator.* It is a rule of human nature that while we are giving our opinion about something, we are developing commitment to the idea. If you want paraeducators to be committed to their work and to the best outcomes for students, ask them what they think about what approach to take with a particular child or what materials they would use. Of course, a newly

employed paraeducator may have fewer ideas. Over time, if paraeducators understand that you want and expect them to contribute ideas about how to do something, they will become more adept at it. They will begin thinking for themselves about how to perform various tasks, in anticipation for the next time you ask. Not asking, just giving a paraeducator every detail, may be faster in the very short run, but probably won't be as effective in the long run because he or she will come to depend on you as the sole source of ideas.

5. *Set deadlines, time frames, and follow-up dates.* Of course, some of the assignments you make don't have a specific deadline; they are ongoing. Usually, we can offer a timeframe—a period of time during which we want the paraeducator to carry out certain types of instruction or student assistance. When paraeducators perceive that a task doesn't have to be done by a specific time or within a certain time period, they may procrastinate or may think it isn't important. Clarifying the timeframe minimizes the chance of miscommunication or conflict. It is also valuable to establish checkpoints or follow-up dates at which time you will review the data on the outcomes of the instruction being provided by the paraeducator, so you can be assured that the delegated tasks are being carried out correctly and that they are having the desired effects. It is natural to forget to follow up and if you don't write it into the schedule or on a calendar, it may not happen.

6. *Specify the level of authority.* This is one of your opportunities to involve the paraeducator and use his or her knowledge, experience, and skills to their fullest. You may decide to give different amounts of authority for different tasks. There are four possible levels of authority. You may need to establish multiple levels of authority for various aspects or functions involved in the task.

For example, Barbara also works with Jamila. She was directed to work one-to-one with Jamila to reinforce the two-digit multiplication her class had been working on, but Jamila didn't seem to understand yet. One day, Barbara unexpectedly found that Jamila remembered exactly how to perform the function and was able to complete all the assigned problems in a few minutes. The teacher who supervises Barbara was not in the room and Barbara had to decide what to do next. Did she have the authority to determine whether she should go on with a more advanced skill, make Jamila continue to practice the same skill, or stop and reward her with a pleasant but unrelated activity? Like the teacher that Barbara works with, you won't always be around when your plans are carried out. Your direction happens at a distance. So what do you do? You consider the possibilities and direct the paraeducator to make certain kinds of on-the-spot decisions in certain situations.

There are four levels of authority:

a. Give the paraeducator the full authority to take action, using his or her judgment, to make whatever decisions seem necessary in the situation.

b. Give the paraeducator the authority to take action, but require him or her to stay in touch and specify how often he or she will stay in touch and who initiates contact.

c. Require the paraeducator to get approval before taking action or moving on to the next step.

d. Require the paraeducator to do only what you tell him or her to do. You might use this level with new employees, entry-level or inexperienced employees, low achievers, or substitutes.

7. *Guide and monitor the tasks.* This delegation step is important to ensure that the paraeducator can effectively carry out the tasks that have been delegated. To do so, the paraeducator must have all the information about the task, the student(s), the materials, and the political realities. Then he or she needs to know what approach to take. While you want to ask the paraeducator's opinion, you must also have ideas and suggestions about approaches that are the most effective to get to the outcomes you want. How should the paraeducator prompt a student who doesn't know and can't decode the words he or she is reading? Finally, a paraeducator must know the intended outcomes. What is the goal of reading orally with a student? What does fluent oral reading sound like?

Like every aspect of delegation, monitoring takes time. Of course, the amount and intensity of monitoring depend on the history of the working relationship. The longer you have known the paraeducator and the more skillful that person is, the less direct monitoring you'll do. Shorter histories or fewer skills means that more intensive, direct observation is necessary. Managing your time well means that you have built time into your schedule for monitoring and feedback to paraeducators. The general rule of thumb in monitoring is to focus on the objectives, rather than the perfect execution of prescribed actions. However, there are times when precise execution of a technique *is* necessary. Identifying such times is easier when precision and perfection are not constant demands. While monitoring paraeducators' work is necessary for ethical practice, it is not necessary to hover over them during every instructional episode (Heller, 1997). In fact, this would be a waste of your time and theirs. In addition, many paraeducators lose self-confidence if you monitor too closely. Communication style and work style differences sometimes result in tasks being performed differently than the planner had envisioned. The professional who delegates tasks should clearly differentiate between idiosyncrasies of style and incorrect performance of a task. Sometimes professionals who are concerned with perfection err by taking a task back prematurely. It is a mistake to short-circuit paraeducator effort before he or she has a chance to improve. If you've chosen the right person and are clear about your expectations, then remind yourself to be patient enough to allow the paraeducator to reach your standards. In the end, this will save time because he or she will be able to do the task alone.

Finally, you will want to note and recognize good performance. Everyone enjoys a bit of praise now and then, but the issue of noting and recognizing good performance goes beyond being nice. Documentation of performance should be specific to the objectives of the task and the specifications of the plan. Even when paraeducator performance is not yet perfect, recognizing improvement gives the motivation to continue to grow and improve.

CHAPTER SUMMARY

Delegation is both a time-taker and a time-saver. It takes organization, time, and skill to delegate well. The investment of time and energy into effective delegation pays off on a day-to-day basis, however, because it frees you to do the things that only a professional can and should do. Your effectiveness grows as your delegation skills grow. Your efficiency at delegation allows you to be the highly ethical, effective professional you want to be.

7 Planning for Paraeducators

THE IMPORTANCE OF PLANNING
FOR PARAEDUCATORS' WORK

There is growing emphasis on student outcomes in this country. The slogan "No Child Left Behind" and recent legislative actions focus our attention on our accountability for student learning. Planning is essential if we intend to achieve excellent student outcomes for typical students. It is even more critical to plan effective curriculum and instruction if we intend to achieve acceptable outcomes for students whose learning doesn't come easily or who are at risk for educational failure.

Dynamic instruction is founded on good planning and good planning is founded on assessment information. While most teachers have stopped using the planning forms their education professors gave them, effective teachers are absolutely clear about the purposes of their lessons and they create classroom experiences that target those purposes. They decide ahead of time what activities they'll engage students in, how they'll provide directions to students, and what materials they'll need at their fingertips. They know what homework will be assigned and they know beforehand how they'll prepare students to engage with the concepts. When well-organized school professionals fail to plan, they may only be able to wing it or make it through a class without disastrous results.

However, when no one plans for the instruction delivered by para-educators, it means that paraeducators, who are unprepared to plan lessons, are on their own to design the instruction. It is unacceptable for a paraeducator to work with students who have complex learning needs, or with social, emotional, or health issues, with no written plan provided by a supervisor. Yet, this is commonly the case. Paraeducators, unfortunately, are frequently allowed to make decisions that should be rightfully and appropriately made by fully qualified professionals. Interviews with paraeducators reveal intuitive attitudes about their role in the planning process, in the absence of role specification. Some paraeducators believe it is their job to keep students with disabilities from bothering the teacher. They believe that they are responsible for all aspects of a child's education, that they have to create all adaptations for the child, and that they are responsible totally for the child. They have been allowed to deliver services with little guidance.

Paraeducators who are placed in such positions realize that they are poorly equipped to do the job. Some paraeducators have reported that, "I make my own plans." Others reported, "No one plans, I just follow along trying to do what I'm supposed to" (French, 1998), and still others reported that they "write lesson plans for the reading group" (Hansen, 1996). Paraeducators in Minnesota reported that they held full responsibility for students, including planning lessons and activities, even though state policies do not advocate such responsibilities for paraeducators. In California, paraeducators also reported high levels of responsibility including complete decision-making responsibility regarding curricular and instructional adaptations and modifications.

When teachers are asked if they plan for paraeducators, they often admit that they don't. Sometimes teachers try to justify their lack of planning for paraeducators, "I don't need to plan, she just knows what to do." Or, they say, "She doesn't need a written plan, I just tell her what to do on the 'fly' " (French, 1998, 2001)." While these responses may reflect the current state of affairs, none of them exemplifies a legal or ethical position.

Should we expect something different from paraeducators than we expect from teachers? In a word, yes. Paraeducators are not teachers. They are valuable school employees who hold a legitimate role in the teaching process, but they work in a different capacity than teachers. For example, paraeducators assist teachers of students who are learning English but they do not have the skills to conduct language assessments or to plan lessons that focus on language acquisition.

Paraeducators also assist special education teachers, but they don't have extensive knowledge of disabilities or of assessment techniques. Similarly, library assistants hold a legitimate role in a school library, but they are not library and media specialists, they don't have curricular preparation, and they shouldn't determine the nature or structure of the library and media collection. Speech-language and occupational therapy assistants carry out related services interventions, but lack knowledge and credentials to practice either of those professions. They should not diagnose or plan the interventions themselves.

We expect nurses and doctors to have different roles. We recognize that a nurse may give the injection to a patient, but we understand that the doctor prescribed it. Nurses do not prescribe medications or courses or treatment—they deliver them. They provide daily care to patients, ensure the delivery of prescribed medications and treatments, and record data so that the doctor can make informed decisions about further treatment. Similarly, we do not want paraeducators prescribing instructional sequences, units, lessons, or adaptations. We do want paraeducators delivering instruction and interventions, carrying out the curricular adaptation plans made by the professional, and recording data so the teacher or other school professional can make informed decisions about further instruction or intervention.

Moreover, even if we hired a paraeducator who happened to hold a particular kind of knowledge, it is still not legitimate to assign a teacher's role to a paraeducator. In this country, we don't allow people to work as beauticians until they obtain licenses to do so. Likewise, paraeducators should not be allowed to assume a teaching role until they hold a license and are hired in a teaching position.

Designing instructional environments and making decisions about the goals, objectives, activities, and evaluations of instructional episodes are tasks that are well outside the paraeducator's scope of responsibility. We should not let it slide when a paraeducator, who works on an hourly basis, with little preparation and no professional credential, is allowed to plan or, worse, is forced into planning for students because the professional has neglected to do so. Paraeducators should not be asked to do the teacher's job. There is an important instructional role for paraeducators, but that does not include usurping the teacher's role. Effective paraeducators require effective guidance (as described in Chapter 6). Effective guidance is only possible where written plans exist. Administrators should hold school professionals to that standard.

Which Professional Plans?

All school professionals hold a responsibility to plan for the students in their class or on their caseload. So, speech-language pathologists plan for all students on their caseload, whether they deliver all the services personally or not. Likewise, a special education classroom teacher plans for his or her own class of students. A bilingual teacher plans for all students in his or her class. The library and media specialist plans for the library and media center. The school nurse plans for the students who are on his or her caseload because of health-related needs.

For special education students who are included in general education classes, it is the duty of the general education teacher to plan lessons and individualized adaptations based on all existing individualized plans for the student and with consultation from all the other appropriate professionals. "With consultation" means that all professionals who are involved with a student's IEP (individualized education plan, or other individualized plan) are obligated to provide relevant information about the functioning of the child in that domain to the general education teacher and to other special education service providers. In addition, it is best practice for a special educator to assist in every way possible when the required adaptations deviate significantly from a typical lesson for that classroom teacher.

Specifically, it is not legal or ethical for a paraeducator to adapt lessons that have been designed by general educators, even though it is perfectly acceptable for the paraeducator to create or revise materials and to carry out the adaptations planned by the professionals. A special education teacher may create a procedural plan to cover several types of lesson activities and tasks that classroom teachers typically employ. The paraeducator may then apply the general modification plan to the specific instructional activity or task on a day-to-day basis.

Adaptations to General Education Curriculum and Instruction

Questions about adaptations arise among teachers who are involved in the inclusion of students whose instructional and curricular needs are not typical. For students with disabilities, there are two laws that provide guidance on the subject. First, IDEA '97 requires that students with special education needs have an IEP and other individualized plans as necessary that include goals and objectives to "enable the student to participate in the general curriculum." In addition, Section 504 of the Vocational Rehabilitation Act of 1973 requires any agency that receives federal funding to afford persons with disabilities the same rights and privileges that persons without disabilities are allowed. This means that all students must have access to curriculum and instruction, even if it requires adaptation. Teachers must provide adaptations to the curriculum or instruction for any student who has a disability, or is perceived to have a disability, whether or not the student qualifies for special education services.

Thus, special education students and students with disabilities who are not in special education must be given access to the same general education curriculum that their peers receive. These laws clearly shift the emphasis of inclusion of students with disabilities in general education classrooms from a social purpose to an academic purpose. Moreover, they elevate the importance of careful planning for adaptations. Now, there is legal accountability for the planning of adaptations and school professionals assume the responsibility for providing such plans to paraeducators.

Yet, numerous researchers report that paraeducators routinely make decisions about adaptations to classroom instruction for individual students when they are assigned one-to-one. This practice has always been ethically questionable, but now IDEA '97 makes it legally dangerous. School professionals hold the responsibility for designing the types of adaptations that are appropriate and acceptable for students with individualized plans and for providing written guidance to paraeducators regarding appropriate adaptations to make on the spot.

The Paraeducator's Role in the Adaptation of Curriculum and Instruction

So, what is the role of the paraeducator in adapting curriculum and instruction? The paraeducator holds the ethical responsibility to follow written plans and oral directions provided by any or all school professionals assigned to the student with disabilities. The written plans need not be complex, but must be developed by the professionals who participated in assessment of the student and in the IEP planning, and who hold responsibility for that student's IEP goals and objectives. A list of goals and the related adaptations covering the range of classroom instructional situations meets the legal requirements if it is shared with the paraeducator as well as general education teachers. The example below is a list of goals with related adaptations that have been determined to be appropriate for Aram, a 6-year-old student who sustained a traumatic head injury. Aram receives the majority of his education in a first-grade classroom and attends "special" classes (art, music, physical education, computers) along with his age-peers. See Table 7.1 for Aram's procedural plan.

This plan, like all good adaptation plans, does not specify who will perform each task, but clearly lays out the kinds of adaptations that must be used. This type of plan could be used as a vehicle to ensure three major communication

Table 7.1   IEP Goals for Aram

IEP Goals for Aram

1. Acquire independence in tasks of daily living

2. Participate in general education curriculum

3. Improve eye-hand coordination

4. Strengthen left side

1st Grade Classroom Adaptations for Aram (based on his IEP)

1. Outline handouts for coloring or cutting with 1/4" marker. Provide hand-over-hand guidance when Aram starts to cut, but reduce guidance as he acquires proficiency.

2. Present materials to Aram to the right of his visual field (because of a left-field deficit approximately 45 degrees from midline).

3. Whenever manipulative objects are used in class, direct Aram to grasp objects and provide hand-over-hand guidance as necessary for him to grasp objects to strengthen his thumb and index finger grasping. As proficiency increases, reduce guidance.

4. Offer bead stringing as an optional activity when Aram has completed assigned tasks or during class times when he is unable to participate in typical instructional activities. The purpose is to practice patterning and to improve visual/motor activities. Encourage independence by using a plastic straw supported with clay on the table. Guide him to use self-talk about the patterns (as directed).

5. Aram's ability to write is limited, so while the rest of his class writes sight words, he writes only one or two words and then changes to the use of letter stamps to put words on paper.

6. Computer adaptations: use enlarged numbers and letters on keyboard and screen.

7. When other students are writing, paraeducator or teacher takes dictation from Aram or assists with the use of a tape recorder to record his story or ideas. As his keyboarding skill increases, replace dictation and tape-recording with keyboarding his ideas.

8. Provide physical prompts paired with verbal prompts. Then, fade the physical prompts and use only verbal prompts when Aram uses the bathroom or is dressing to go outdoors to encourage his independence in removing and replacing his elastic waist clothing.

9. Use verbal prompts to remind Aram to keep his left hand on the tabletop or to use both hands when carrying objects. Remind him to self-monitor and use self-talk.

10. Whenever other students are working on activities on the floor, put Aram in a prone position on hands and knees and ask him to pick up or manipulate objects with his right hand. This encourages him to put weight on his left side and build strength on that side. Make a game of it, involve other children, to avoid the appearance of Aram being different.

---

components. First, it provides a source of written communication from all special education professionals to the first-grade teacher. Second, it provides a vehicle through which the special education teacher or case manager communicates with the paraeducator about Aram's specific needs for which he receives special education services. Third, it serves as the basis for communication between the first-grade teacher and the paraeducator. The first-grade teacher plans curriculum and instruction for all her students, including Aram, and then turns over certain materials, schedules, plans, and activities to the paraeducator to carry out. As Aram grows older, his goals and objectives will change. So will the types of classroom instruction and activities. The plan will need to be adjusted periodically to meet his changing needs. However, the planning is not overly demanding because the frequency of revision is not great—possibly only once per year. Therefore, the kind of plan that a paraeducator needs for carrying out curricular and instructional adaptations can be in effect for a long time and does not need to be rewritten very often.

Communicating About Student Progress

In addition to the three communication features of the procedural plan, a fourth type of communication is also important. That is, communication about the progress of the student. An effective procedural plan includes some method for written communication between all the adults that work with a particular student. For example, Aram's plan could have a place on which the paraeducator or classroom teacher could make specific note of his response to adaptations, the instructional opportunities he experienced, and his progress toward IEP goals. Table 7.2 shows how Aram's adaptation plan might include the fourth communication component.

HOW TO PLAN

Planning Variables

Because the tasks that paraeducators perform vary substantially in complexity and risk, the type and level of planning also varies. Some of the planning variables to consider include the following.

Paraeducator Experience, Skill, and Training. If a paraeducator has performed the same type of instructional activity, student supervision assignment, clerical task, behavior management technique, data collection, or health service in the past, and has performed satisfactorily, then plans may be very brief. A sentence or phrase added to the schedule would suffice. On the other hand, if a paraeducator is new to the position, has received only a brief training, or doesn't have the skills, the plan must be more detailed, specifying outcomes, actions, materials, cautions, and levels of authority.

Complexity of the Task. Obviously, clerical work requires minimal planning and direction, but instructional work requires more. The more complex the instruction, or the intervention, the more important it is to give specific directions in

Table 7.2   Aram's Daily Communication Sheet

Date: _____

Goal Numbers	Adaptation Number/Used for_____ ☐	Level of Independence	Prompts Provided
1, 2, 3	1. Outlining/reading worksheet—cut and paste	mod	PP
2, 3	6 & 7. Keyboarding during writing time	min	PP
4	10. Lying on carpet—during storytime—Aram signaled answers to teacher questions with his right hand	max	VP
	Anecdotal Comments: This is a real step forward for Aram—he really did more of the cutting than ever ◄──┘ before. Keyboarding required significant physical prompting—probably close to 95% but not quite 100%		

NOTE: Dep., dependent (100% paraeducator); Min., minimum independence (75% paraeducator, 25% Aram); Mod., moderate independence (50% paraeducator, 50% Aram); Max., maximum independence (25% paraeducator, 75% Aram); Indep., independent (100% Aram); VP, verbal prompt; PP, physical prompt.

the plan for data recording, use of language, and instructional techniques. For example, a paraeducator should be given specific directions regarding the amount of student success or failure to tolerate. A paraeducator may be directed to allow a student to fail at a task and then redirect his or her efforts or, alternatively, to give enough prompts and cues so that student performance is errorless. In the case of a bilingual program, the paraeducator needs to know which language to use with students, whether to translate instruction or not, and how to provide student supports. Behavior issues are also complex. A paraeducator working with students who have significant behavior or social issues needs more guidance about appropriate ways to interact with the students, appropriate limits to set, and types of behavior to tolerate or ignore, as well as the behaviors that require interruption, redirection, or reinforcement.

Risk. Two circumstances that increase risk are structure and distance. Structure refers to the circumstances of the situation. Where there are walls and doors, where the activities are performed uniformly with other students, and where there is little movement or few choices, there tends to be less risk. Distance is the physical separation between the paraeducator and the person responsible for the outcomes of instruction. Where the paraeducator performs his or her work matters. The distance of the paraeducator from the supervising professional is one factor that contributes to risk. The greater the distance, the greater the risk. Greater risk requires more specific guidance. For example, Ruby works one-to-one with an elementary school student with autism in the general classroom, hallways, lunchroom, and playground—all at some distance from the special education teacher. Ruby needs full information about the student's health, academic needs, appropriate adaptations, and appropriate instructional techniques, as well as specific directions on how to cue the student to engage in activities. The plan should tell Ruby how much or little verbalization to use and how to work around the student's sensitivities to touch and other sensory inputs.

Another example is of a secondary special education program where students go into the community for life-skills experiences, vocational exploration, or work experience. The paraeducator is working in a high-risk situation, away from the teacher, and in a low-structure situation. Such a paraeducator should have a list of precautions and emergency procedures, as well as specific goals and directions for the instructional sequences that take place in the community setting.

Components of Plans

Good plans are brief, easy to read at a glance, and relatively easy to write. They also contain certain key components (Box 7.1). A good plan specifies how to do the task, the purposes of the task or lesson, the specific student needs to be addressed or strengths on which to capitalize, the materials to use, and the type of data needed to determine whether the student achievement is satisfactory, moving in the right direction, or unsatisfactory. It is also important for the paraeducator to understand how the task fits into the broader goals and outcomes for the student. For example, James, a student with severe and multiple disabilities, has been learning to raise and lower his left arm. If Lu, the paraeducator who works with him, understands that James is preparing for a communication device that depends on this skill, she will be sure that he practices many times a day and that he practices correctly. So, the plan may tell Lu that the goal is for James to raise and lower his left arm deliberately. It should also tell her that the long-range goal is that he will be able to use a button or switch that controls an assistive speaking device. The plan also needs to have a place to document the number of opportunities he had to practice the skill, the amount of cueing or prompting he required to perform the skill, and the number of times he successfully performed the skill, with or without cueing or prompting.

BOX 7.1
_____

COMPONENTS OF PLANS

1. Purpose of task, lesson, or adaptation

2. Long-term student goals, short-term objectives

3. Specific student needs / strengths

4. Materials / resources

5. Sequence of actions, use of cues or prompts, permissible adaptations

6. Data structure for documenting student performance

Communicating About Plans

Unless the plan is communicated in a format that both parties understand in the same way, it is difficult to know whether students are achieving their outcomes. Good planning formats are easy to use and user-friendly. If the planning form or format is handy, is simple, and includes all key components, you will improve your communication and minimize the amount of time you spend doing it. How can you be sure the paraeducator knows how to carry out the plan? You may also need to check for understanding about the plan. Asking the paraeducator if he or she has any questions is one way to open the opportunity for clarification.

Planning Forms and Formats

Plans do not necessarily adhere to a predetermined format. Many professionals (and teams) use their creative talents to design forms and formats that respond to the unique characteristics of their own situation. Professionals have sufficient latitude to create a planning form or format that pleases them and addresses the combined needs of the team. What is contained in the written plan, the amount of detail, and the specificity of directions are all negotiable.

Although a paper-based planning form isn't necessary and plans certainly may be written on any type of surface (chalkboards, dry-mark boards) or electronic platform (handheld electronic planner, centrally located computer), school professionals tend to rely on paper. Using blank paper means that the plan writer will have to write certain pieces of information or structural aspects of the plan over and over again. Forms eliminate the duplication of effort and streamline the planning process. Paper-based planning forms, like other planning formats, must also meet the dual tests of ease-of-use and user-friendliness.

Ease-of-Use

Ease-of-use means that the plan form or format should be readily available and comprehensive enough to cover all the key components, yet simple enough that the professional can use it consistently. The professional is the best judge of ease-of-use. For example, a template created and kept on a word processor may be readily available for a professional who has a computer on his or her desk. Multiple copies of a printed form kept in a desktop folder may be easier for another professional. Length of the form is also important. Too many components make it difficult to know what to write and too tedious to write it in each space. Including too few components may result in the transmission of too little information or of information that is too general to be useful.

User-Friendly

User-friendliness refers to the visual appeal of the form and its familiarity. User-friendliness is best judged by the paraeducator. Visual appeal often means that there is a lot of white space or graphics on the page and that the length is sufficient but not overwhelming. A paraeducator faced with a two- to three-page plan will be less likely to read the plan carefully than he or she would given a single page, neatly written or typed. The use of common terminology and a reading level that is consistent with the knowledge and literacy level of the paraeducator are also important factors in user-friendliness.

Building Your Own Planning Forms and Formats

As you begin to design your own planning forms, you may want to use some of the following ideas. The examples shown in Tables 7.3–7.6 show various layouts and designs for components of planning forms. They all meet the two tests of ease-of-use and user-friendliness and they contain all necessary components. To create your own forms, combine the styles you prefer from the options. Make sure all the key components are included. You may also need to add other components depending on the program and specific family or student needs. In early childhood special education programs, plans may be based on individual family support plans (IFSPs). In K-12 special education programs, plans are guided by IEPs, individual health plans (IHPs), or individualized behavior plans (IBPs). In Title I programs, plans are guided by literacy assessment information and, in the case of students with limited English proficiency, language assessment information. Students with disabilities that do not qualify for special education services may have a 504 plan.

Table 7.3 shows a plan form for Sean, who has a mild learning disability. In this situation, the paraeducator is assigned to a series of general education classrooms because students who need curricular and instructional modifications and adaptations are placed in those classrooms. Sean is just one of those students. Classroom teachers teach their classes as usual, but the special education teacher has taught the special education students some strategies that they are supposed to apply in their classes. The paraeducator provides support for the students to ensure that they are using the strategies they've been taught. So, in addition to Sean's plan, the paraeducator would also carry plans on a clipboard for each of the other students she monitors.

As you examine the contents of this plan, you may notice that there are abbreviations with which you may not be familiar. For example, the terms RAP, 2-Column Notes, QAR, TOWER, and STOP[1] represent specific strategies the teacher has taught to Sean. The important thing is that the paraeducator who works from this plan *does* know what RAP, 2-Column Notes, QAR, TOWER, and STOP are, how to coach students in the use of each strategy, and how to cue students to use them at the appropriate time. The teacher who made this plan either taught the paraeducator about the strategies or knew that the paraeducator already possessed that skill. The form includes a table for collecting data about Sean's progress using the strategies he's been taught. The paraeducator completes the form each day for two weeks and then files this form in a notebook on the teacher's desk. The teacher is able to adjust plans or reteach skills as necessary because she has current information about Sean's performance. Finally, the teacher periodically monitors to see that the paraeducator is using the cueing systems appropriately.

Table 7.4 is a form that could be used when the paraeducator is assigned to work with a single student in an inclusive situation, a pullout situation, or a

Table 7.3

Lesson Plan for Application of Modifications and Adaptations for
  Student: _Sean_   Classes: _English, Math, Social Studies, Science_

IEP Goal: Sean will become more independent at academic tasks by applying learning strategies

Learning Weakness: Strategy deficient   **Learning Strength:** Visual processing

Short-Term Objectives for Core Academic Classes:
1. S uses RAP strategy to paraphrase information from the text
2. S uses 2-column note-taking strategy for note taking during lectures
3. S uses QARs for finding answers in written materials
4. S uses TOWER strategy for theme / essay writing
5. S uses STOP strategy to self-monitor his understanding of directions

Special Materials:
1. Cue cards for all strategies previously taught in special education class

Paraeducator Tasks:
1. Give verbal prompt if S needs to employ a strategy but has failed to do so spontaneously
2. If he is unable to determine which strategy to use, provide all cue cards to remind him of choices, ask him to select appropriate strategy, note # of prompts necessary
3. Assist S in using strategies as necessary, note inappropriate use of strategy
4. Ask S to repeat the directions to you for assigned tasks

Documentation Key:

Strategy Used (RAP, 2-CN, QAR, TOWER, STOP)

SAS, Selected Appropriate Strategy   AUS, Appropriate Use of Strategy

IUS, Inappropriate Use of Strategy   I, Independent

P, Prompts

Date	1/3	1/4	1/5	1/6	1/7	1/11	1/12	1/13	1/14	1/15
Eng										
Math										
SS										
Sci										

resource room. This plan happens to be for a student with significant cognitive needs and limited social functioning. Ashley is included in a fifth-grade classroom for much of the day, but is pulled out to the resource room for frequent but short periods to work on various communication and academic skills. In this case, the location of the "choices" activity is varied so Ashley will learn that she can make choices in lots of places throughout the day. This plan is good for a long period of time, but the team will vary their directions just a little in subsequent months and thus reuse large portions of the written plan. For example, the goal statement and sequence of the activity will be the same next month but the activity choices will change. The team finds that using a planning form makes them very efficient. They don't have to rewrite everything every week. This is especially important because it is not the only plan they make for Ashley. There are also procedural plans for how she will work and what she will do every period of the day. Notice the section in the plan that specifies the objectives for Ashley's friends. This is a unique feature of this team's planning format. In this situation, the team is trying to educate typical students to provide some of the support for Ashley so that the adults don't isolate her from her age-peers. The special education teachers negotiated with the fifth-grade teacher to release several designated students to work with Ashley as part of a circle of friends.

The team added the friends' goals' feature to the planning form when they noticed that the fifth graders were overprotective and tended to do too much for Ashley. They realized that to achieve her social goals they had to teach the other students how to work with her. So, whenever Ashley is pulled out during these periods of the day, certain of her friends are assigned to accompany her and the paraeducator has clear direction on what they are to learn from the experience.

Table 7.5 contains a form that could be used by a Title I or an ESL teacher to provide directions for working with a small group of students who are practicing specific language or vocabulary. This type of lesson plan format is appropriate for paraeducators who work in pullout rooms or in general education classrooms. As in all plans, the paraeducator must understand how to complete all aspects of the lesson. This lesson happens to be about basic vocabulary recognition for students in seventh-grade science. The teacher who wrote the plan asks the paraeducator to ensure that students are using a memory device called Keyword.[2] It is not important for the paraeducator to know or understand the learning theory that is the basis for the Keyword technique, as the teacher does, but it is necessary for the paraeducator to know how to explain it to students and to give good examples. Thus, the paraeducator must be trained and coached to deliver this lesson. The most important feature of this planning form is that it includes a structure for the paraeducator to provide feedback to the teacher who holds the ultimate responsibility for the outcomes of strategy instruction and student strategy use in classes.

A special educator in Colorado who supervises nine paraeducators developed the form in Table 7.6. Each paraeducator works one-to-one with students who have significant and multiple disabilities. In this example, a student named Calvin has communication and physical goals that are being addressed throughout the day in various classrooms. When the paraeducator comes in

Table 7.4   Ashley's Pullout Activity Plan

Timeframe: _____

Goal: To understand that she can choose among activities but that once she makes a choice she has to stick with it for a period of time.

Sequence of Activity:

1. Ashley makes a choice from the choice book

2. Ashley selects the materials she needs for that choice from the shelf

3. Ashley sticks with the choice she made for 10 minutes

4. Ashley stops the activity when the timer rings

Time Period(s): Frequently throughout every day—whenever an opportune moment arises

Location: Vary location daily

(special education classroom, library, computer lab, 5th-grade classroom)

Activity Choices:

1. States puzzle

2. Simple machines activity box (ramps, levers, pulleys)

3. Alphabet cards

4. Name game

5. Choices that other 5th-grade students make

Friends' Goals:

1. Cue Ashley to make choices and get materials

2. Redirect Ashley when she gets off task

3. Cue Ashley to stop when bell rings

	Activity Choice #	Gets Materials	Attends	Stops
M				
T				
W				
Th				
F				

Enter activity choice number, level of assistance required for making choice, getting materials, attending, and stopping
V, verbal prompt
PP, physical prompt
HOH, hand over hand
NA, no assistance

each morning, she picks up a clipboard with a blank form to be completed as Calvin goes through his day. She has received prior instruction on the adaptations appropriate for Calvin in each of his classes, and the classroom teacher provides additional direction during class. During unstructured times, such as bus loading and unloading, transition from class to class, and lunchroom, Calvin has specific objectives to be addressed through routines and activities. The paraeducator is responsible for Calvin's engagement in those activities and for documenting his performance.

Schedules

Schedules tell when tasks should be completed, who should perform the tasks, and where people are during the day or week. They are often developed simultaneously with lesson or work plans and provide a graphic display that accompanies the specific information contained in the lesson or work plan.

Table 7.5   Vocabulary Procedures for Seventh-Grade Students

Objective: Students will read and define vocabulary words with 100% accuracy using a keyword device.

Activity:

1. Students sit together at round table

2. Show one card at a time

3. Say "what is this word?" and "what does it mean?"

4. If students gives incorrect response, or can't respond, say "This is _____ , it means _____." Then help student generate a keyword memory device to recognize and define the word.

Materials: Prepare 3 x 5 file cards with the following words on one side and the definitions on the other. (Use definitions from life science text.)

Student Performance: Record performance

Key: R = reads it correctly/date   D = defines it correctly/date

	Radius	Ulna	Humerus	Tibia	Fibula	Femur	Pelvis	Scapula
Taneesha								
Hugo								
Nikolai								
Kiely								
Soua								

Table 7.6   Calvin's Communication, Academic, and Physical Activities

1. Calvin will use his communication device to communicate a want or need

Classroom Activity	Total Trials	Number Independent	Number Assisted	Assistance Type

2. Calvin will make a choice between a like and a dislike using his communication device

Options Presented	What Calvin Chose	Number Independent	Number Assisted	Assistance Type
/				
/				
/				

3. Calvin will greet peers using his communication device

Message	Times Played/Opportunities	Type of Assistance (circle)			
Hello		PP	HOH	Verbal	No assistance
What's up?		PP	HOH	Verbal	No assistance
Hi		PP	HOH	Verbal	No assistance

Table 7.6 continued

4. Calvin will use sign or gesture to communicate

	Level of Prompting		
Current Words	Hand over Hand	Verbal	Independent
Food			
Drink			
Bathroom (need to go)			
All done			
Stop			

5. Goal: Calvin will eat lunch unassisted

Current Objectives	I	Min.	Mod.	Max.	Dep.
Get spoon					
Scoop					
Lift to mouth					
Clear utensil					
Return utensil to plate					

6. Goal: Calvin will participate in typical classroom activities

	Classroom Activity	Calvin's Activity
Hour 1 Occupational Skills		
Hour 2 Communication		
Hour 3 Choir		
Hour 4 Personal Skills		
Hour 5 Lunch		
Hour 6 Computers		
Hour 7 Life Skills		
Hour 8 P.E.		

7. Goal: Calvin will get on and off bus unassisted

	I	Min.	Mod.	Max.	Dep.
Off (am)					
On (pm)					

Anecdotal messages from school:

Messages from home:

Key:
I = Independent
Min. = 75% Calvin
Mod. = 50% Calvin
Max. = 25% Calvin
Dep. = Dependent

While the plan answers the questions "What does the paraeducator do?" and "What does the student do?" the schedule answers only the questions "When?" and "Where?"

It is most useful to have schedules that include information about all team members. It is also useful to display schedules publicly so that the information is readily available to others. Like plans, schedules can and should reflect the unique needs of the team and the circumstances. The unvarying features include times, locations, and activities of all team members. Table 7.7 contains one example of a schedule form used at a middle school. In this case, the whereabouts of the teacher and the paraeducator are publicly available and a notation telling what they are doing during each time block is included. The schedule does not tell the nature of the activity, the goals, or the materials used in lessons or classes. That information is contained in related plans.

CHAPTER SUMMARY

Too often, no one plans for paraeducators. When this happens, paraeducators are on their own to design and deliver instruction. Good plans have

Table 7.7   Daily Schedule

Time	Paraeducator Activity / Location	Teacher Activity / Location
8:00–8:10	Meet bus, take Ian to locker, then to first class	Plan with Social Studies teachers or Social Studies Office
8:10–8:40	Resource Room – strategy instruction	Resource Room – strategy instruction
8:40–8:50	Accompany Eric to PE from Room 38 to gym	Resource Room – strategy instruction
8:50–9:20	Support Jason, Michele, Tanya, Roy in Room 44	Coteach with Smith in Room 29
9:20–10:05	7th-grade Language Arts group in Resource Room	Coteach with Smith in Room 29
10:05–10:30	Plan time in Special Education Office	Plan time in Special Education Office
10:30–10:50	Accompany Eric to Health Room for respiration treatment and medication Take Eric to music class	Coteach with Jones in Room 44
10:50–11:25	Lunch	Coteach with Jones in Room 44
11:25–11:50	Computer lab	Plan with Language Arts teachers in Language Arts Office
11:55–12:25	Taneesha, Hugo, Soua, Kiely, Nikolai in Room 44	Testing/consultation/IEP meetings

common features including purposes, goals, or objectives; student needs and strengths; materials and resources to be used; sequence of actions; use of cues or prompts; and permissible adaptations; as well as a structure for documenting student performance. Plan forms should be easy to use and readily available to the professional, as well as user-friendly for the paraeducator. Schedules are necessary companions to plans, providing the locations and times for various activities of both professionals and paraeducators.

NOTES

1. QAR stands for question-answer relationship. It is a way for students to recognize that certain kinds of questions demand certain kinds of answers. The use of QAR helps students know how to formulate answers differently according to the demand of the question and the source material they are using to find the answer. RAP stands for read-ask-paraphrase. Students read a selection, ask themselves about the main idea, then state it in their own words. 2-column note-taking is a technique students use to put the main topic or idea in one column and the details in the other. TOWER stands for think, organize, write, edit, revise. Students use the strategy to write papers. STOP stands for stop, think, and plan. Students use it to monitor their own thinking and behavior in a variety of situations.

2. Keyword is a method where the learner links a word with a definition by constructing a mental image or drawing of a scene that includes the word itself and illustrates the meaning of the word. As with any other skill, students must be taught to understand and use the keyword method.

8 Paraeducator Training

IDENTIFYING TRAINING NEEDS

Individual Needs

Planning for paraeducator training occurs initially during orientation, as discussed in Chapter 5. The initial planning identifies the training needed by an individual paraeducator and is based on the assessment of paraeducator skills and confidence levels in comparison to programmatic needs. Gaps are noted and an initial training plan is created. The plan indicates the type of training needed for the task, the competency or skill desired, possible trainers, and when the training is needed. This initial plan reminds the teacher about the kinds of on-the-job training he or she will need to provide. It also suggests other possibilities for training, such as having another, more experienced paraeducator provide the training to the newcomer or providing videotaped material, Internet resources, or written materials. It also identifies the need for more formal classroom-based training because not all training can or should occur on the job.

Group Needs

Needs assessments are the most commonly used tool for identifying the preferences and desires of the intended audience and provide information about where to start your training program for the paraeducators in your school or district. The term *needs assessment*, however, can be a bit misleading. The natural inclination is to think that you are identifying all the training that paraeducators need. Beware of this subtle difference. While needs assessments do provide some sense of preference and give you some insight into what paraeducators already know about their training needs, they cannot possibly identify all the training needs of people who do not yet have experience with all the possible knowledge or skill they may need. For example, paraeducators may say that they need information about disabilities, but they may not recognize that they also need to develop skills in adult-to-adult communication. Some skills such as interpersonal communication may be more readily identified by their supervisors. It pays to view the results of needs assessments cautiously.

The most effective needs assessments are designed with the roles and responsibilities of paraeducators in mind, not leaving the most obvious training needs to chance. A sample needs assessment is contained in Table 8.1. For a training curriculum that addresses all the needs identified in this needs assessment, visit the Web site of the PAR^{2}A Center: www.paracenter.cudenver.edu.

Table 8.1   Paraeducator Training Needs Assessment

Areas in Which Training Is Needed	Now	In the Future	Never
Team Roles			
Team communication and functioning			
Roles and responsibilities			
Ethical and legal responsibilities			
Adult communication			
Effective working relationships			
Conflict management			
Problem-solving steps and processes			
Stress management			
Instruction			
Following lesson plans			
Implementing curricular adaptations			
Levels of support for students			
Getting the attention of students			
Maintaining active student participation			
Basic mathematical concepts			
Math computation skills			
Using public transportation systems with groups of students			
Math standards			
Creating instructional materials			
Helping students select reading material			
Make arrangements for field trips			
Create forms for parental permission and fee collection			
Techniques for reading to and with students			
Facilitating reading comprehension			
Reading standards at the state and district level			
Written language skills			
Developmental process of written language			
Engaging students in organizing and producing written language			
Written language standards at the state and district level			
Instructional Technology			
Operate audio-visual equipment, copy machines, fax machines, computers			
Augmentative communication systems			
Recognize high- and low-tech speech devices			
Create low-tech communication devices			

Table 8.1 continued

Areas in Which Training Is Needed	Now	In the Future	Never
Behavior			
Principles of behavior modification			
Functions of behavior			
Teaching rules, procedures, and routines			
Data recording and reporting			
Principles of communication with students			
Management strategies for minor behavior problems			
Facilitating friendships among students			
Define behavior in terms that students can understand			
Direct instructional methods to teach behavior			
Contingency reinforcement			
Teach rules, routines, and procedures for small or large groups of students			
Behavior management techniques			
Antecedents, behaviors, and consequences			
Logical and natural consequences that are positive and nonaversive			
Redirect, reframe, and reinforce behaviors			
Purposes for data collection			
Use data recording forms			
Duration and frequency data			
Special Education			
Special education laws			
Legal rights of students with disabilities			
How students qualify for special education services and 504 plans			
Steps and processes of special education services			
Values and rationale for inclusion of students with disabilities			
Disability categories			
Needs of students with disabilities			
Distinguishing facts from myths about people with disabilities			
People first language			
Accessing information about disabilities, syndromes, and medical conditions on the Internet			
Human Growth and Development			
Concepts of human learning			
Students at risk			
Typical language development			

Table 8.1 continued

Areas in Which Training Is Needed	Now	In the Future	Never
Health and Safety			
Health, safety, and emergency procedures and practices			
Maintaining physical health and safety of students			
Reporting child abuse, suicidal ideation, or other illegal or dangerous behavior			
Health-related care in school settings			
Medically fragile children			
Role of the school nurse			
Delegation of health-related procedures and the paraeducator role			
Cultural Diversity			
Identifying culturally based habits and patterns			
Communication characteristics of English speakers and non-English speakers			
Diversity in cultural heritages, life styles, and value systems			
Personal Growth and Development			
Self-analyses of job-related skills			
Choices for training opportunities			
Self-evaluation methods			
Using constructive feedback and criticism from supervisors			
Plan for self-improvement			
Student Supervision			
Lunchroom safety precautions and first aid specific to choking and aspiration			
Signals for getting students' attention in the lunchroom and playgrounds			
Eating procedures for students with special eating needs			
Natural supports for students with special needs			
Teaching prosocial lunchroom behavior			
Rules and instructional methods for typical playground games			
Safety precautions for children using playground equipment			
Teaching prosocial playground skills			
Principles of playground supervision			
Establish rules, routines, and procedures for bus riding			

Table 8.1 continued

Areas in Which Training Is Needed	Now	In the Future	Never
Maintain order on the bus			
Emergency safety procedures			
Bus operation procedures			
Mediate conflicts among students on the playground			
Playground peer mediation programs			
Instructional Technology			
Development of communication			
Assertive technology			
Adaptive equipment			
Computer use for instruction			
Transition Programs			
Transitioning students to vocational or career training			
Employment or career-training options and vocational programs			
Career planning			
Marketing and job development			
Job site analysis			
Self-determination for students			
English Language Learners			
Laws and court rulings regarding English language learners			
Education services for English language learners			
Working with students who are learning English as a second language			
Programs for English language learners			
Understand how cultural differences affect teaching and learning			
Helping newcomers adjust			
Second language acquisition			
Factors that influence language acquisition in schools			
Instructional methods used in bilingual classes			
When to use the first language and when to use the second language			
Strategies and techniques used in sheltered English instruction			

Planning to Deliver Formal Training

The second consideration in planning for paraeducator training is how to provide the core knowledge, competencies, and skills required by everyone who works with students. Formal classroom-style training is a preferred mode for numerous aspects of instructional knowledge and skills. All the findings of research on staff development for teachers also apply to training for paraeducators. When planning paraeducator training, there are several concepts to keep in mind regarding the delivery of training.

Adult Learning Principles

Obviously, paraeducators are adult learners. This is an important consideration because, unlike children, adults cannot be coerced into learning something they believe is irrelevant, useless, or trivial. In other words, adults must want to learn and they will learn only what they feel a need to learn. Therefore, making paraeducator training problem based and realistic helps paraeducators see how the concepts apply to their own work situation. Paraeducators are typically working parents who have limited time to spend in training sessions. They have little need for tasks that are strictly academic and less practical (e.g., writing term papers, taking tests). While it is always advisable to plan a variety of methods and structures when preparing training for adult learners, keep in mind that paraeducators often learn best in a less formal environment that allows them to incorporate discussion and questions. Finally, while many paraeducators are not college graduates, they typically come to the job with skills and knowledge gained through child rearing, life experience, other jobs, and other types of training. Effective training and trainers recognize and capitalize on the prior knowledge and experience paraeducators bring to the job.

The Content or Curriculum for Paraeducator Training

Another essential consideration is the content of paraeducator training. To understand the particular training needs of paraeducators, a review of the paraeducator role is important. Paraeducators teach, but they are not teachers. They do not plan instruction, design curriculum, determine curricular adaptations, assess students, or maintain responsibility for reporting on student progress. Therefore, the training they need does not necessarily include information about planning, curriculum design, determining types of adaptations needed by students, assessment techniques or methods, or progress reporting materials.

At the core of an effective training program is a curriculum that is coherent and complete. The curriculum for all paraeducators needs to include information about teamwork, problem-solving skills, and conflict management techniques because paraeducators work as part of a team composed of professionals and paraeducators. It also needs to include information about how to follow unit and lesson plans provided by professionals, because their teaching is planned by and directed by the teacher or related services provider. They need specific techniques for managing large groups of students in unstructured situations such as bus loading zones, hallways, lunchrooms, and playgrounds because they spend many hours in those situations. They need training in the use of mature interpersonal communication skills because they take direction from many different adults with innumerable communication styles. They need background knowledge about the variety of routines, procedures, and rules teachers employ to manage groups of students because they step in and out of various classrooms and instructional environments throughout their day. They need training in the use of specific research-based instructional techniques (particularly in reading, language, and mathematics instruction) because they spend the majority of their day providing individualized instruction and tutoring small groups of students. They need to understand the principles of behavior management as well as the current thinking about behavior support approaches that teach socially acceptable and appropriate behaviors to students. Paraeducators also need skills in reflection and planning for their own personal growth and development.

For paraeducators assigned to specific programs, additional training in job-specific skills may be necessary. For example, paraeducators working in special education need specific information about the nature of disabilities and the implications for language development, communication skills, social development, academic skills, and health. Paraeducators in English language learning programs obviously need additional preparation in basic concepts of English language learning, second language acquisition, literacy, and teaching methods. Health room assistants require training in administering medications, CPR, and first aid, reading individualized health plans, and maintaining health records.

Paraeducator Training Materials

There are several sources of training materials currently available for paraeducators. The materials, however, are not of equal quality. Some materials provide inappropriate instruction, unnecessary instruction, or incorrect information, or advocate a particular point of view. The following 10 principles should guide the selection of commercial materials. Table 8.2 provides a convenient checklist by which to rate commercial materials you are considering.

Need. Curriculum should emphasize knowledge, concepts, and skills paraeducators need in their current work situation. Selecting curriculum appropriate to need requires a careful job analysis and a clear recognition of what paraeducators are being asked to do. For example, a paraeducator working in a secondary transition program probably needs training in transportation safety for students in the community, job coaching, environmental analysis, and workplace safety, whereas a paraeducator in a developmental preschool program is more likely to need information on toilet training, nutrition, cognitive development, social awareness, and language development in young children.

Consistency. Content of the materials should be consistent with the philosophy and mission of your school. Avoid selecting materials that prepare paraeducators to work in a setting that is unlike yours. Some video materials cur-

Table 8.2 Curriculum and Materials Analysis

Consideration	Curricula						
	1	2	3	4	5	6	7
Need[a]							
Consistency[b]							
Integrity[c]							
Relevance[d]							
Depth[e]							
Role legitimacy[f]							
Practicality[g]							
Instructional quality[h]							
Accountability[i]							
Cost[j]							

a. Knowledge, concepts, and skills paraeducators need in a particular assignment
b. Matches the philosophy and mission of your school or program
c. Accuracy and honesty
d. Curriculum addresses skills essential to the paraeducator's assignment
e. Amount of time and number of activities related to a particular skill or concept
f. Coverage of concepts, skills related to legitimate roles and responsibilities
g. The immediate applicability of the skills or concepts
h. Has specific goals and objectives, instructional materials
i. Specifies competencies gained by paraeducators and how they are measured
j. Expense in time, money, human resources, or knowledge necessary to use curriculum

rently available show scenes from a self-contained program where a teacher and a paraeducator share a classroom with only 8 to 10 students. Paraeducators working in inclusive environments will recognize little of their own situation in those scenes.

Integrity. Content of the materials should be accurate and honest. Errors or inaccuracies detract from the usefulness of the materials and present an unnecessary dilemma for instructors. Watch out for biases and personal agendas disguised as common practice. Look for research-based practices that include the best of what is known in instruction.

Relevance. The curriculum should address skills that are essential to the paraeducator's assignment and avoid teaching skills to paraeducators that are not legitimate parts of their jobs or are not relevant to paraeducator assignments in your district. The key is to consider the actual and legitimate roles and responsibilities of paraeducators. Using materials that teach unnecessary skills to paraeducators wastes time and money.

Depth. Related to relevance is the depth of the training materials. Depth refers to the amount of time and number of activities related to a particular skill or concept. If you expect a paraeducator to perform a skill, or if you believe that a particular concept is fundamental, you can legitimately expect to spend more time teaching that skill than you spend on knowledge-level material. Analyze the materials you are considering to determine whether the depth matches your expectation. Lecture material or casual mention of a concept or skill may not be sufficient to prepare a person to perform that skill or understand the concept to the degree you expect.

Role Legitimacy. The curriculum should emphasize the importance of relying on the teacher or related services provider to communicate the direction of the instruction. Role legitimacy refers to the inclusion of knowledge and concepts that specifically relate to the legitimate roles and responsibilities of paraeducators and avoid teaching skills that would allow a paraeducator to do the job of a teacher. Materials that seem to place the paraeducator in a decision-making position or that ignore the rightful supervisory role of the teacher are inappropriate. Check to be sure the materials prepare the paraeducator to follow and clarify directions, to participate as a legitimate and important team member, but not to usurp the authority of teachers. Look for materials that emphasize ethical behavior, mature communication, problem solving, and conflict management skills as well as classroom instruction skills.

Practicality. The curriculum should be practical and problem-focused, and should not involve extensive theoretical material designed to educate scholars or prepare researchers in the field. Practicality refers to the immediate applicability of the skills or concepts. Numerous articles attached to the materials that are intended to be used as reading assignments or for writing research papers should raise a red flag. Paraeducators are technicians, not scientists—they require know-how and application-level materials rather than theoretical frameworks.

Instructional Quality. Curriculum materials should include demonstration materials, practice activities, opportunities for trainees to get feedback during the training session, and recommendations for coaching as well as lecture material. Instructional quality is measured by the presence of specific goals and objectives that tell what outcomes the paraeducator will achieve, background information for instructors, handouts, transparencies, directions for activities, and discussion guides. Materials that ignore the best practices of paraeducator training should be avoided.

Accountability. Accountability means that curriculum materials specify the competencies and skills that will be gained by participating paraeducators and how those can be measured or observed. These specifications should allow you to document skills for which the paraeducators can be held accountable after training. This provides a basis for performance monitoring and evaluation later on.

Cost. Cost is always important to consider. Look carefully at what you get for the amount of money you will pay. Consider the related costs of delivering the training as well as the initial investment for the materials. Consider whether the materials are self-administered by paraeducators and whether that will achieve the outcomes you want. Some self-administered workbook-type materials are available at no cost online. In this case, it pays to consider whether you will be able to document the competencies and skills paraeducators have gained through training.

Consider the costs of paying instructors to deliver the training. Also consider the human resources you have available to deliver the training and whether those individuals could pick up the materials and use them without further preparation. If the materials involve contracting with a university or college instructor or outside consultant consider the cost in both time and travel dollars, release time for paraeducators, and honorarium payments. Distance learning materials and Internet-based classes have become popular in recent years, but may require special equipment, space, or prerequisite technology comfort and skills on the part of the paraeducators. These factors become part of the overall cost of a training package. Before investing in any materials or packages, be sure that you can afford the types of costs associated with it. The worksheet in Table 8.1 can be used to quickly assess training materials you examine.

DELIVERING TRAINING TO PARAEDUCATORS

Paraeducators deserve the best training we can provide. Years of research on staff development for teachers have resulted in the identification of five essential training components: theory, demonstration, practice, feedback, and coaching. There is little doubt that these training components apply to the training of paraeducators as well as teachers. Although the training components are discreet, each component builds on the prior one.

Theory

Theory means that the skill, strategy, or concept is clearly explained or described. While paraeducators do not require significant amounts of learning, language, or behavioral theory, they do need honest, straightforward information about the basic concepts so they will have a context to understand why and when they will use certain instructional, behavioral, literacy, social, and language learning techniques. Presentation of conceptual information is, however, rarely enough for paraeducators to be able to apply information to the job. Table 8.3 shows how each of the training components builds on the other with theory as the foundation.

Teachers tend to receive much more theory in their preparation because the teaching role requires substantial decision making about instruction and behavioral approaches, curriculum planning, program design, and student assessment. Teachers sometimes say that they had too much theory and too little of the other training components in their own preparation. If this is true, it provides a healthy warning to those who are planning paraeducator training to not repeat the mistake.

Table 8.3   Relationship Between Impact of Training Efforts and Training Components

Training Components	Paraeducator Learns and Understands the Concept or Disposition and Recognizes the Skill	Paraeducator Can Demonstrate the Skill When Asked	Paraeducator Applies Concept or Skill on the Job
Presentation of theory	85%	15%	10%
Demonstration or modeling	85%	18%	10%
Opportunity to practice and get low-risk feedback on skill performance	85%	85%	15%
Coaching	90%	90%	90%

SOURCE: Joyce and Showers (1980).
NOTE: Interpretation: If demonstration or modeling is used as part of the paraeducator training session, 85% of the paraeducators will understand the concept or skill, or understand the disposition or belief, that is being proposed. Only 18% of them will be able to demonstrate the skill or will show evidence of having changed their attitudes, beliefs, or dispositions as the result of the training. And, only 10% of them will be able to apply the concept on the job. If on-the-job coaching is added subsequent to the training session, about 90% of the paraeducators will understand the concept *and* will be able to demonstrate the skill, attitude, or disposition when asked, *and* will be able to apply the concept or skill on the job. Coaching is the most powerful of all the training components in terms of skill application.

Demonstration

Demonstration means that a skill, strategy, or concept is modeled or shown in some way, so the trainee sees, hears, or touches an example or sees how it works in real situations. For example, a video could be used to show how to lift a child out of a wheelchair without sustaining back injuries. Or, the teacher might model the use of prompts and cues while working with a child, differentiating between the two as she uses them and showing how to systematically decrease levels of prompting at the same time. This component is essential if the paraeducator will have to perform the skill with students. As is evident in Table 8.3, without demonstration, the conceptual or theoretical information is useless to most learners.

Practice and Feedback

Practice means that the paraeducator tries out the skill, strategy, or concept in a controlled or safe place—probably not with students. Often that place is in the classroom where the training session is taking place. Practice can take many forms. When teaching conceptual information, it may mean discussion with a partner about how the concept applies in the real world. For example, when teaching the principle of normalization for students with disabilities, the instructor can guide a discussion of how those principles are demonstrated in the use of age-appropriate instructional materials, instruction of social behaviors, students' schedules, and so on. In another example, a workshop or class on literacy instruction may include the concept of using authentic children's literature. When paraeducators have the opportunity to look at children's books and contrast the language in them with the language of vocabulary-controlled texts, they will understand the concept and be able to understand why the teacher may have selected one over the other.

In a class on assisting in classrooms with English language learners, the instructor may explain the problems associated with simultaneous translation of instruction and demonstrate how a paraeducator would engage students in a supplemental discussion of the content in their native language after the teacher's instruction in English. However, with only that much information, paraeducators may be unable to lead such a discussion. If they are given multiple practice opportunities on various instructional topics, a paraeducator is more likely to be able to perform that way in a real classroom.

Feedback means that the instructor provides information to the trainee about how well the trainee performs the skill or strategy or understands the concept. For example, during a practice activity on a social skills instruction sequence, the instructor stops a paraeducator who forgets one step in the sequence and offers a cue that serves to help the paraeducator remember how to present information to students. The instructor then watches the complete instructional sequence a second time and points out how the paraeducator was able to complete the sequence independently. When added to the training session, practice with feedback substantially boosts the learning of participants and increases the likelihood that the paraeducator will be able to demonstrate the skill when asked.

Coaching

Coaching is an essential part of the training, but typically occurs after the training session, on the job, while the paraeducator works with students. Coaching involves watching the paraeducator perform the skill or apply the concept on the job, with students or team members, and providing useful feedback so that the paraeducator can refine his or her use of the skill or application of the concept as a result. Often, the teacher performs this aspect of training because it melds with performance monitoring.

As shown in Table 8.3, coaching is the most powerful of all the training components, yet it tends to be the one that is least used. Why? Coaching takes supervisory skill, requires time, and therefore is more costly than other training components. It does almost ensure, however, that the skill, attitude, or disposition will actually be applied in the classroom. Without coaching, we have little assurance that training efforts will pay off in terms of student achievement or improved performance of paraeducators.

Details of Holding Paraeducator Training Sessions

Conducting paraeducator training sessions involves numerous logistical details that fall into five categories: paperwork, facility, identification aids, people, and presentation aids. Table 8.4 can be used as a convenient checklist to ensure that all the details have been considered.

Paperwork

Paperwork includes information sheets or advertising fliers, attendance sheets, a roster of those who preregistered, agendas, and evaluation forms. Attendance records should be retained as documentation of training.

Facility

Arranging for a facility in which to hold the training is a first step. Your district may have training facilities that can be scheduled, but if not, a suitable room should be found. It pays to confirm the facility as the day draws near and to identify at that point the safety and comfort features of the facility such as lighting and sun control, heating and cooling adjustments, ventilation, and the

Table 8.4   Details of Paraeducator Training Checklist

Paperwork
- _ Information sheet
- _ Advertising flyer
- _ Attendance sheet
- _ Preregistration roster
- _ Agenda
- _ Evaluation form

Facility
- _ Facility scheduled
- _ Facility confirmed
- _ Identification of safety and comfort features
  - _ Lighting, sun control, heating, cooling, ventilation adjustments
  - _ Telephones, exits, restrooms

Identification Aids
- _ Nametags
- _ Table tents
- _ Signs

People
- _ Introducer
- _ Speaker
- _ Technical support person
- _ Facilities contact person
- _ Catering
- _ Housekeeping contact
- _ Registration assistant

Presentation Aids
- _ Transparencies
- _ PowerPoint presentation
- _ Handouts
- _ Samples and examples
- _ Easel, newsprint, flip chart
- _ Marker pens
- _ Tape
- _ Scissors
- _ Stapler
- _ Paper clips
- _ Pens and pencils
- _ Pointer
- _ Extra handouts
- _ Slides and blank transparencies

location of telephones, exits, and restrooms. If your budget permits and you are serving beverages or food, it pays to review the details of the plan for making them available to participants.

Identification Aids

There are several reasons to preplan and use identification aids in training sessions for paraeducators. Premade nametags can be placed alphabetically on a registration table for participants to pick up as they enter. This becomes a form of sign-in. Those who do not show up are immediately obvious to the organizers. In addition, the use of nametags permits the presenter to address people by name and allows paraeducators to learn the names of other paraeducators. An alternative to nametags is table tents, folded paper with the names of participants on them, placed on tables in front of the respective participant. Table tents may be used as a supplement to nametags and are particularly helpful to presenters when a group is very large and the typed or printed names are small.

Directional signs are helpful to hang in strategic locations for participants who are not familiar with the facility. Signs help direct traffic, guiding participants to restrooms, entrance doors, refreshments, telephones, or other comforts.

People

A list of key people helps organize the training event and ensure that all will proceed smoothly. You probably want to include the person who will introduce the event, welcome participants, or establish the importance of the event as well as the speaker or presenter. Other helpful people to have on the list are a technical support person who can assist in the event of equipment malfunction and a facilities contact person to assist with room temperature, lighting, ventilation, sound control, seating capacity, and so on. A catering or housekeeping contact is useful when food or beverages are served and for supplies that may run short. It is often helpful to have someone assist with registration and with transition times so that event organizers can be available to participants during transitions.

Presentation Aids

Most presentation aids, such as transparencies, PowerPoint presentations, handouts, samples, and examples will be developed ahead of time and often prepared by the instructor or presenter. You may want to keep the following presentation aids on hand during a presentation or class even if they have not been identified ahead of time: easel, newsprint, marker pens, tape, scissors, stapler, paper clips, pens, pencils, flip chart, pointer, extra handouts, slides, and blank transparencies.

Evaluating Paraeducator Training

Participant evaluations are important for a variety of reasons. Evaluation forms completed by participants immediately following a session tell us how much and what they think they learned. They also tell us how the participants perceived the content and the delivery of the session. Evaluations tell us how participants perceived the physical and psychosocial characteristics of the session, as well as their attitudes, beliefs, and dispositions about the content. Evaluation forms can be used to elicit suggested improvements from the participants.

However, evaluation forms have significant limitations and the results of evaluations conducted immediately after a session should be viewed cautiously. For example, evaluation forms cannot assure us that the participants learned the content as we intended. They cannot predict how much of the instruction will be applied in the classroom or school, nor can they ensure that there will be improvements in student outcomes. Most important, evaluation form ratings do not predict whether attitudes, beliefs, and dispositions existing at the conclusion of the training session will continue after participants return to work.

Evaluation forms are for stakeholders to take an immediate reading on the success of the training event. They are summative in that they are completed at the conclusion of the event. Evaluation forms may present negative information and may give discontented individuals permission to air their grievances. Whether the feedback is positive or negative, having the information makes it possible to improve the content or the delivery in the future. Remember, evaluation forms and the comments written on them can be difficult, even devastating, for the presenter if criticisms are presented rudely.

Documenting Paraeducator Training

There are many reasons to document the training provided to paraeducators. First, paraeducators are more valuable to the district, school, program, or classroom when they acquire more skills. They also deserve to be recognized and honored for increased skill levels as their value to the district increases. Without documentation, however, it would be impossible to fairly recognize or dignify the training paraeducators have received. Therefore, it makes the most sense to maintain group records, organized by training session, and individual records, such as transcripts, showing the training that each paraeducator has taken. Group records are easily gathered at the training session in the form of a roster of attendees or a sign-in sheet. Together with a course description or training outline, this information would constitute adequate documentation. A transcript-like form for documenting an individual's training is shown in Table 8.5. Of course, if the training carries college credit or is provided by a college or university, transcripts are automatically provided for each paraeducator. Arranging for college credit or contracting with a college to provide training would save the time and cost of this step.

Second, documenting paraeducator training is an important safeguard. Sometimes a paraeducator doesn't meet the employment standards or is a poor performer. In this case, termination may be an eventual consideration. It is more expensive to terminate and rehire than it is to provide training. Therefore,

Table 8.5 Paraeducator Training Transcript Form

Paraeducator Name:	
Home Address:	
Telephone:	
School and Program Assignment:	
Position Title:	
Social Security/ Employee Identification Number:	

Training Session	Date(s)	Instructor Name	Coaching Date(s)	Name of Coach

it makes sense to begin by providing training, including the important coaching component, and then documenting the efforts.

The third reason for documenting the training you've worked hard to provide is to demonstrate that you are protecting the safety and welfare of students by training those that monitor them in unstructured situations and provide instructional support, discipline, health care assistance, advice, guidance, and direction. Parents and families of children expect that their children are safe at school and schools need to assure them that they are. Documentation of training is one way of providing such assurance.

Finally, the documentation of training provides a basis for legal defense if necessary. A legal defense may become important if a child is injured or mistreated in any way because of the actions of a paraeducator. Showing that the paraeducator has received training that is appropriate to his or her job responsibilities and that the training covered safe and ethical behaviors may absolve the district of legal responsibility for actions outside those prescribed in training sessions and save money otherwise spent on a legal defense.

CAREER DEVELOPMENT FOR PARAEDUCATORS

This nation faces a teacher shortage. This is one of the reasons for the increased use of paraeducators. Certain aspects of education are facing critical shortages including bilingual education and special education—programs serving students who are at risk for educational failure. It is increasingly true that districts are hiring emergency credentialed teachers to meet the growing student population and to fill the gaps left by retirements and attrition.

Paraeducators have been named as the most potentially recruitable group of people to become teachers. There are numerous reasons for this. The most important and compelling of these reasons are that paraeducators typically live nearby and are a part of the community. Often, they share the native language and culture of the families served by the school. Paraeducators tend to begin their employment in schools during the years that they are raising their children, thus tending to be a bit more mature than the typical beginning teacher. Also, unlike younger, more traditional teacher candidates, paraeducators already know and understand what it is like to work in a school, so working conditions will come as no surprise to them. Finally, because paraeducators already work for extremely low pay, teaching salaries look attractive by comparison.

Recruiting paraeducators into teaching careers is not necessarily easy, however. By definition, paraeducators are not traditional college students. Many paraeducators did not attend college at age 18 and may have had many different reasons for not seeking higher education. For some, marriage and family responsibilities took precedence. For others, there were limited financial options, little encouragement, and a lack of guidance. In some cases, minority paraeducators were discouraged from becoming teachers by guidance counselors or teachers believed they had little chance of succeeding in college. Others simply lacked confidence in their own scholarship or academic abilities.

"Grow-your-own" career ladder programs have been developed in local school districts that are particularly affected by teacher shortages in specific areas. This approach is highly feasible because administrators and teachers already know paraeducators. Their intuitive skills and ability to work with others are obvious to those around them. For these reasons, administrators and teachers are in prime positions to identify those paraeducators who show potential for being excellent teachers.

Yet, because they are nontraditional college students, paraeducators who intend to become teachers have unique needs during their teacher preparation programs. The research in this area clearly demonstrates that grow-your-own career ladder teacher-preparation programs are highly successful in preparing excellent teachers. Moreover, the success of such programs can also be measured in the retention of teachers who completed such programs. Retention rates after six years of teaching often exceed 95%, unlike more traditional teacher candidates who show much lower retention rates and high levels of attrition in the first three years of teaching.

Recruitment

Success begins with recruitment of potentially excellent teachers. Successful programs tap into an existing pool of paraeducators presently employed by a school district who are already highly committed to the field. They look for paraeducators who show good intuitive skills, a willingness to grow and learn, and the ability to work well with other adults in a collaborative style, as well as those who believe that all children can and will learn.

Financial Support

Financial support is an important feature of programs that prepare para-professionals for teaching careers. The types of financial support vary substantially across programs. Some programs actually administer and provide scholarships, grants, or tuition reimbursement for courses completed with acceptable grades. Other programs merely locate scholarships, loans, and forgivable grant programs for paraeducators and assist with application procedures. However, financial assistance alone does not guarantee that para-educators will persist toward completion of their teaching license.

Cohort Classes

Cohort classes refers to the practice of starting a class-sized group of para-educators in a teacher-preparation program at the same time so they take classes together and proceed through the program as a group. For many para-educators who lack confidence in their academic ability, cohort groups provide safety. They know that they are among friends and colleagues and they are encouraged to share ideas and to rely on one another for emotional and academic support. In addition, cohort classes provide opportunities for students to commute with one another, thus alleviating some of the costs associated with travel to and from the college campus.

Cohort Group Meetings

Cohort meetings are often advising sessions with topics that include time management, stress management, and information about state licensing standards, testing, college requirements, and other topics of mutual interest and concern. Cohort group meetings allow paraeducators to talk through problems and concerns, get questions answered, and arrange tutorial support or assistance with assignments as well as emotional support.

Tutorial Support

Some paraeducators have excellent potential, but lack some of the basic academic or study skills to succeed in college. For those paraeducators, tutorial support is necessary to learn skills they missed in their earlier educational experience. Some paraeducators experience anxiety about certain subjects (e.g., math) and sometimes have weaknesses in areas such as written language. Tutorials provide prereading of papers and assistance with editing. For para-educators who learned English as their second language as children or adults, the use of academic forms of the language is especially difficult. Assistance from native English-speaking editors is a critical element in learning to use academic English.

Likewise, some native English-speaking paraeducators who want to work in bilingual education have obtained tutorial support in the language they are acquiring as a second language. Their cohort members often provide opportunities to speak the second language with a native language speaker.

Flexible Course Schedules

The most obvious difficulty for working adults is that typical teacher preparation programs occur during the workday, assuming that college students have a source of support that permits full-time attendance during the day. For paraeducators, who typically work a six- to seven-hour day, scheduling classes on weekends and evenings makes it possible for them to persist in the program. Individuals have different preferences, of course, but flexible scheduling may permit other family members to assume child care and household responsibilities, freeing the paraeducator to attend class. Certain religious and cultural preferences of cohort groups should be considered in the scheduling of courses.

Mentoring Program

The mentoring program provides opportunities to connect with a teacher at the school in which he or she works. Mentoring is a highly personal arrangement, but good matches of mentors and "mentees" provide someone to talk to about problems in class, with assignments that involve applying skills on the job. Mentors really care about the paraeducators they are helping educate. Master teachers have much to share with novices and, in many cases, mentoring allows them to demonstrate their excellence and how years of hard work have paid off. In many ways, they become the role models for paraeducators. It is difficult to administer an effective mentoring program because not all relationships work smoothly. Sometimes a mentor teacher and a paraeducator don't make an ideal match and the relationship is terminated. It takes administrative skill to help both individuals recognize that good people sometimes don't hit it off.

Practicum Experiences

Most programs require participants to complete field experiences that transition the paraeducator into the teacher role. While paraeducators have substantial teaching and student supervision experience by this point of the program, they often lack experience with curriculum and instructional planning, assessment, program direction, paraeducator supervision, and accountability.

However, field experiences are not easy to arrange. Because paraeducators are already working, and are usually dependent on their income, they cannot afford to take time off to complete a traditional student-teaching experience. Some paraeducators are able to complete practicum in a summer program, assuming the teacher role, directing others, and taking full responsibility for the class. Some grow-your-own programs provide a paid field experience during the academic year, continuing paraeducators on their current pay scale throughout the field experience period so they don't suffer the loss of income.

Family Support

As working adults, paraeducators experience stresses that are different from those of younger, typical college students. While they rarely are concerned about having a date for the dance, paraeducators find that time pressures keep them from spending quality time with their children and spouses. In some cases, this problem spawns family dissension. Spouses' concerns grow as the demands of the program increase and cause change in the family's lifestyle. Certain cultural characteristics as well as relationship styles contribute to the problem.

Family activities, initially designed as informational meetings for spouses and children, help the family connect with the paraeducator's life as a student. These family activities permit spouses to meet, share fears and concerns, and find solutions to the stresses imposed on the family by a member who is in a teacher-preparation program. As a result of family meetings, many long-lasting friendships have been formed and social relationships go beyond the scope of the program. Families in similar situations bond with and support one another.

Program Director

A program director or adviser is essential to a successful grow-your-own program. The role of the director involves negotiating systems adjustments that individual paraeducators would be unable to do. For example, the role includes providing help with registration, negotiating the financial aid system, course and program advising, and finding appropriate tutoring and counseling if necessary. Without guidance, many paraeducators would fail to complete the program, just as many typical 18-year-old undergraduate students fail to complete their education because of a lack of guidance.

The program director also negotiates within the school system on behalf of the paraeducators. For example, interim raises that honor the progress of paraeducators toward a teaching license have been negotiated by program directors. Managing the mentor program and supporting good mentor-mentee relationships are essential to the success of that aspect of the program. Time to complete field experiences does not happen automatically and must be arranged by the program director. Program directors make the arrangements and plan for the family support activities and cohort group meetings.

CHAPTER SUMMARY

There are three types of paraeducator training. First, on-the-job training provided to individuals by teachers is essential to get a new paraeducator started and is identified during orientation. Second, formal training is necessary for paraeducators to perform optimally. Needs assessments provide information about training needs for paraeducators as a group. Training sessions must be carefully planned and organized to achieve the desired outcomes. Finally, some paraeducators have the potential to become excellent teachers, filling the need for increased numbers of teachers. The training and support needs of these paraeducators are different from those of typical college students and 10 program components ensure success for paraeducators who pursue teaching careers.

9 Monitoring and Evaluating Paraeducator Performance

MONITORING PARAEDUCATOR PERFORMANCE

Monitoring a paraeducator's performance of assigned tasks ensures that they will be done correctly and on time. When the other elements of supervision such as orientation, careful planning, scheduling, training, delegation, and direction are already in place, monitoring is the next logical step. The word *monitoring* implies observation. Observation of paraeducator task performance and behavior is essential to performance monitoring and to the feedback and evaluation processes. This means that the teacher must take five minutes here and there to watch the paraeducator doing his or her work. Long observation periods that would be burdensome to the teacher are unnecessary. Twelve five-minute observations give more information about performance than a single observation of an hour. Of course, this means that the teacher has to recognize that observing the paraeducator is a legitimate use of his or her time and must accept that he or she will have to step outside an instructional role for a few minutes at a time.

For teachers to begin to see themselves in this role, administrators must first recognize that responsibility for monitoring the work of paraeducators is legitimately within the teacher's role. Then, the administrator must hold the teacher accountable for the performance of paraeducators. At the same time, teachers need substantial support in this area, because it is an area in which few teachers have experience or training. Moreover, it is an area that may be contested by paraeducators if teachers begin monitoring, coaching, and providing feedback and there is no precedent for teachers in that role.

Support for teachers in this role requires two things of administrators. First, it requires that administrators hold teachers responsible and accountable for their programs, just as team leaders in businesses are held accountable for

145

the production of their teams. Second, it demands that administrators provide support to teachers in terms of on-the-job training, coaching, and feedback to teachers on their supervisory skills.

Observation Techniques

There are two primary observational methods. One is an unfocused observation, in which the observer is prepared to look for any of the skills or tasks that have already been assigned to the paraeducator. Usually, unfocused observations are used when there has been no preplanning and when the observer has no particular skill or behavior in mind. Focused observations, on the other hand, are used when there has been specific on-the-job training, conversation, or coaching on particular skills or tasks.

Unfocused Observations

An unfocused observation might consider personal style components, such as use of voice, gestures, or nonverbal communications. An unfocused observation could just as easily focus on the content or organization of the lesson or the materials. It might be about the interactions the paraeducator has with students, the paraeducator's use of behavior management techniques, or time management. In a sense, an unfocused observation is like a wide lens on a videocamera. It picks up many different simultaneously occurring events and takes in all it sees. There is no preplanned, intended focus for an unfocused observation. While conducting an unfocused observation of a paraeducator, the teacher might take notes on events, script the conversation between paraeducator and students, or draw diagrams of movement in the room.

For example, Marion, a teacher, finished instructing her class and started the students on their assignment, and then moved over where she could observe Sharm, a paraeducator, who had been assigned to a group of students doing catch-up work. Sharm carried the grade book with her, reminding each student about assignments that were missing from the grade book and helping them look through their folders for the missing work. She moved from desk to desk, helping one student find the right page to complete an unfinished math assignment and then turning to another student and giving the next word on the spelling test. Marion watched, making notes about what Sharm said to students and drew a diagram using a continuous line to show how Sharm was walking around among the students. She placed Xs in the spots on the line where Sharm stopped for more than 30 seconds or so to talk to a student or look over the student's shoulder.

In this case, Marion collected three types of data in just five minutes. She noted what Sharm did (walked around students, touching, using her proximity to maintain their attention, demonstrated "with-it-ness"). She also wrote down the exact words Sharm used when she offered encouragement and praise to students, and she diagrammed Sharm's movement around the students. All three types of data will be used to inform her feedback and coaching with Sharm later on.

Focused Observations

A focused observation, on the other hand, involves some preplanning phase that identifies what the focus will be. Once the focus is determined, a checklist or form may be selected or developed to address the particular focus. For example, if Marion had been talking to Sharm about the use of open-ended questions as a way to get students to respond more completely, the focus of subsequent observations might tally the total number of questions asked during an observation and the number of them that were open- or closed-ended. A checklist simply identifies the presence or absence of a particular behavior. Another technique, called scripting, involves writing down all the words that are spoken, verbatim.

Scripting is useful when trying to capture the interactions between paraeducator and students. For example, scripting all the words spoken in a short period of time can be used to examine the ratio of student talk to adult talk. It is difficult, as many administrators know, to keep scripting very long because the rate of speech tends to be much faster than writing. Scripting loses its power as a feedback tool when even a few words are left out.

Selective verbatim is sometimes an appropriate alternative. Like scripting, it captures the spoken words and interactions but, unlike scripting, it focuses on certain, preselected events such as questioning levels, frequency of questions, and clarity of directions word-for-word. Often principals and other administrators who have been trained in supervisory methods are familiar with these observation techniques, but most teachers are not. When administrators coach teachers in the use of observational techniques, they are optimizing the supervision of paraeducators.

Documenting Observations

Observations are important to the performance monitoring and summative evaluation processes, so they must be documented systematically. Each observation should have some type of paper associated with it. A brief narrative summary, typed or handwritten, would be fine. Copies of the data collected during the observation would also be worth keeping in a file. If nothing else, a checklist of observation dates for each paraeducator on crucial skills would be useful.

PROVIDING FEEDBACK

Like employees in any business, paraeducators need ongoing or formative feedback on the performance of their job duties. Teachers can provide formative feedback to paraeducators that is based on observations of the tasks assigned to the paraeducator via the personalized job description. Formative feedback helps paraeducators develop new skills and improve current skills because it tells them what they are doing correctly and what they are not doing satisfactorily. Moreover, formative feedback, by definition, is provided frequently throughout the school year, allowing time for paraeducators to increase their use of satisfactory behavior and to improve unsatisfactory behavior. Formative feedback is thus essential to the coaching component of paraeducator training explained in Chapter 8.

Formative feedback and the observations that fuel it become the basis for summative evaluation because the teacher contributes that information to the administrator who holds ultimate responsibility for paraeducator evaluation. The school administrator then completes the formal performance evaluation based on the data collected by teachers and related services personnel.

Formative Feedback

There are five guiding principles for providing formative feedback.

1. *Performance.* Feedback must be directed toward performance rather than personal characteristics. Performance refers to the actions of the individual on tasks that have been previously assigned, taught, and coached. Personal characteristics are qualities an individual possesses that are not assigned, taught, or learned. Such things as height, weight, voice quality, facial features, mobility, intelligence, sensory deficits, athleticism, and health are personal characteristics that should not be the focus of performance feedback. For example, Sharm, a recently employed paraeducator, is receiving feedback from the teacher regarding her ability to pull together small groups of students, get them to attend, and get started on a task. If Marion, the teacher, says, "Your voice is just too soft and mild to get the attention of the students, they just don't pay attention to you," she is referring to a personal quality rather than the performance of a learned behavior. It makes more sense for Marion to say, "Because you have a soft voice, I've noticed that students don't immediately hear you or pay attention when you ask them to come to you. You will need to stand where you are highly visible to students and project your voice, without using a harsh tone, in order to get students' attention." This kind of feedback doesn't ignore Sharm's personal qualities but doesn't focus on them. Rather it suggests a method or technique for getting the job done in spite of whatever personal characteristics are involved. The focus is on the behavior, not the personal quality.

2. *Specificity.* Effective feedback is specific rather than general. Specific feedback names the behavior in operational terms and then states the value or lack thereof in terms of accomplishing the intended outcomes. For example, Marion observes Sharm during a group activity reinforcing students' use of money and making change. Students are sitting around a kidney-shaped table, taking turns buying and selling classroom objects such as pencils, erasers, chalk, books, and tablets using real money. One student, Will, is sitting on Sharm's right side, very close to her. As Marion watches the lesson proceed, she notes that Will seems to be easily distracted and frequently turns from the activity, even though the activity is of high interest and appeal to the rest of the students. Will leans to his right, picking at something on his shoe. Each time Will leans over, Sharm, without missing a beat, reaches out with her right arm and gently puts it around Will's shoulders and brings him back upright and turns

him toward the group. She doesn't look at him, scold him, or make an issue of his behavior. She just regains his attention when he is distracted and encourages him to rejoin the activity.

Later, when Marion meets with Sharm, she tells Sharm what she saw. Then she explains, "When you gently but firmly put your arm around his shoulder and regained his attention, you not only helped him stay engaged, but you conveyed some important information to the other students. You see, sometimes students who are easily distracted are warned and scolded for their inattentiveness. When that happens, the other kids begin to form opinions about the student, he loses esteem in the eyes of his peers, and the other students sometimes believe that it is okay for them to make fun of him or embarrass him because the adult did. Your action, on the other hand, served to enhance Will's standing in the eyes of the others because you avoided embarrassing him and at the same time used what looks like a gesture of affection. That kind of unobtrusive behavior management is highly consistent with our philosophy here. Your actions show me that you truly understand how we treat students here."

Specificity means describing the behavior clearly, without bias or judgment. When Marion provided feedback to Sharm on the study hall observation, Marion first described factually what Sharm did before she explained the value or quality of the action. She said, "I saw you walk over to a student at his desk and heard you ask him if he had found his math assignment yet." After she had described the behavior she added, "By keeping track of what each student needed, you helped them make the most of the study hall. Sometimes students have trouble focusing on what to do first and they waste time. Your direction and assistance helped them be productive." This description tells what Sharm did and what she said. It first reflects behaviors rather than Marion's attitudes or beliefs.

In contrast, an attitude or belief statement regarding Sharm's actions might sound like, "Sharm you are so good the way you work with these kids." Such statements fail to give the paraeducator specific enough information to know what behaviors to do more of and what behaviors to stop. Maybe it makes her feel good, but feeling good isn't the point. Helping her improve her practice is the point.

3. *Honesty.* Honest words say it like it is. Straightforward, yet tactful, information lets the paraeducator know where he or she stands. Sometimes, teachers are so concerned about maintaining a good relationship that they are afraid to be honest. For example, Karen worked with a paraeducator, Allie, who was frequently late to work. The problem with the lateness was that a student who needed assistance getting off the bus and into the building was stranded every time that happened. Yet, Karen wanted Allie to like her and was worried that if she said anything, Allie would distance herself and treat her coldly. The honest way of dealing with the situation would be to describe the behavior, then explain what problem it caused, and finally to ask for different behavior. It might sound like this. "Allie, you arrived after the buses unloaded today and Cooper was left on the bus until the driver came inside to get me. That was a problem because I was on the phone with a parent scheduling a conference at

the time. Please make sure you arrive before the buses in the future, so Cooper will be able to safely get off the bus." There is no point in bringing up past events, even if this one duplicates those in the past. Every event should be dealt with honestly as a separate incident. Only when reminders have been provided on two occasions is it necessary to begin documenting the behavior and the feedback on paper. This kind of feedback is considerate of the needs of the para-educator because it doesn't criticize her or reflect on her character; it just lets her know what behavior is expected and why.

4. *Frequency*. Frequent feedback means daily communication about small things and at least quarterly feedback for an overall look at performance of the skills listed on the personalized job description. Because observations can be as little as four or five minutes, it becomes possible to conduct several observations each week. Frequent observations provide substantial material for frequent feedback conversations.

5. *Consistency*. Consistency refers to the feedback information the paraeducator receives from various professionals with whom he or she works. To provide consistent feedback, it becomes necessary for the professional members of the team to communicate about the paraeducator's performance and share reports of their observations. In the case described above, Allie had reported to work late on several occasions, compromising Cooper's safe departure from the bus. If the occupational therapist, Lisa, who works with Cooper fails to mention that Allie's late return from her lunch break also is a problem, and only focuses on the creative ways that Allie works with Cooper, the feedback that Karen has given may be undermined. In Allie's eyes, her lateness isn't a big problem and she may begin to see Karen as the problem rather than her own behavior. Thus Karen and Lisa need to become more consistent in discussing Allie's lateness with her. They need to work together to find solutions to the problem, so the child's safety is protected. If they fail to work together to provide consistent feedback, Allie's behavior may not change.

In each of the five principles of formative feedback presented above, an underlying current, or theme, is that feedback must be connected to the tasks assigned in the paraeducator's personalized job description. There is no point in giving feedback to a person if the task for which you are providing feedback is not an official responsibility. If the feedback contains corrective information or is perceived as negative, no matter how skillfully delivered, one of the natural reactions of a paraeducator is to defend his or her actions. One common defense that is not easily overcome is that the paraeducator was never assigned or trained for that responsibility. Failure to recognize this basic fact leads to arguments, grievances, and sometimes legal action.

The Role of the Administrator in the Formative Feedback Process

Providing formative feedback is not an easy task, especially since teachers may not have entered the profession expecting to hold this responsibility. The skills required to provide effective formative feedback can be acquired, but first the teacher must understand that it is a legitimate expectation of the teacher's role. The building or central office administrator can do three important things to legitimize this responsibility in the eyes of the teacher.

First, administrators must adjust or renegotiate teachers' job descriptions to reflect teacher responsibilities as program, classroom, and school leaders in which the supervision of paraeducators is a part. Teachers cannot be expected to perform responsibilities or to acquire the skills to perform tasks that are not assigned to them. Then, once it is established that leadership and supervision are important aspects of the teacher's job, evaluation of teacher performance must follow the job description. Therefore, legitimizing the role of teacher as leader and supervisor means that teachers' evaluations should include their ability and skill in maintaining a program and supervising paraeducators.

Second, administrators should mentor and support the teacher in performing supervision of paraeducators. Guidance, suggestions, direction, and advice are appropriate for teachers who are acquiring new supervisory skills. Building administrators, in particular, have taken coursework on supervision and perform teacher supervision as part of their role. Principals are thus the natural coaches and mentors for teachers as they assume new roles.

Third, the roles of teachers and administrators should be carefully delineated. While teachers maintain responsibility for the seven responsibilities detailed in Chapter 3 (orientation, planning, scheduling, delegating, on-the-job training and coaching, monitoring task performance and providing formative feedback, and managing the workplace), administrators take over when it is time to complete the summative evaluation for the paraeducator. Evaluation of paraeducators is the rightful responsibility of the school administrator.

PARAEDUCATOR EVALUATION

There are five facts about paraeducator evaluation that guide the process. First, school professionals (teachers and related service providers) often contribute the data necessary for summative evaluation and performance ratings of paraeducators. This is because they work most closely with the paraeducator and have frequent opportunities to observe the paraeducator's work. They also provide the formative feedback to the paraeducator regarding the daily performance of duties. Therefore, it is important to systematically arrange for teachers who observe paraeducators to provide summaries of formative feedback and coaching sessions, the data that have been collected during observations, and other anecdotal information to the building or program administrator who is the legitimate evaluator.

Second, evaluation is a process by which high-quality work is recognized. This is a universal truth about employee evaluation, so it can be applied to both teachers and paraeducators. A well-functioning, high-quality classroom, Title I program, special education program, library and media center, health room, or lunch program depends on the people in both positions functioning at high levels of proficiency. A building administrator is in the unique position to notice and recognize both the supervisory efforts of the teacher and the performance of the paraeducator. While criticism has its place for those employees who fail to improve their performance in spite of formative feedback that praises their efforts to perform well and coaches them in the performance of their duties, most evaluation should note the positive aspects of an individual's performance. The adage that everyone should be criticized because everyone has something to improve is outdated and counterproductive. People perform best when they know specifically what they are doing well, are praised for their efforts, and are encouraged to continue working in that direction.

Third, evaluation is a process by which the need for training or coaching is recognized. While recognizing the effectiveness of an individual, sometimes weaknesses are also noted. The first order of business for a building administrator with evaluative responsibilities should be to identify the training or coaching needs that will help the employee improve his or her performance. This truism also applies to both teachers and paraeducators. As teachers observe paraeducators, they should note areas in which further training is necessary and make recommendations to the building or program administrator for further paraeducator training.

Fourth, fair evaluation is based on

- Facts rather than opinions

- Standards rather than interpersonal comparisons

- First-hand knowledge rather than hearsay

- Multiple data collection points

Facts are derived from observations of task performance. First-hand observations should be conducted frequently across the school year and should generally be short. The person who is closest to the paraeducator's work and the person who knows it best should conduct observations. Teachers can learn to conduct observations of the paraeducator's work and can find the time to do so if they recognize it as a legitimate part of the job. Frequent, short observations are tucked into the schedule as teachers move from place to place in the building. For example, Marion often observes Sharm on her way back from the gym after she has taken students to their PE class. The classroom that Sharm works in at that time of the day is in the hall near the gym, so Marion drops in for four or five minutes, takes notes, and quietly slips out. She talks with Sharm about it later in the day. First-hand knowledge obtained through this type of frequent, short observation of task performance forms the foundation of a fair, summative evaluation for Sharm.

Standards for paraeducator performance are established early in the process, during the development of the personalized job description. In the personalized job description, tasks assigned to paraeducators are named. These tasks then serve as the standard for performance. It certainly makes little sense to evaluate an individual in comparison with another. Productive evaluation rates an individual in comparison to the tasks he or she has been assigned, trained, and coached to perform.

During formative feedback, the quality of performance is referenced and on-the-job training and coaching are offered for the improvement of para-educator performance. The data collected by the teacher during observations, the documentation of formative feedback sessions, and the documentation of on-the-job training and coaching provide the basis for the administrator's summative evaluation of paraeducator performance.

Fifth, evaluation requires judgment. The emphasis in the previous section on describing observed behavior in operational terms leads to this point. Judgment and opinions about the value or quality of the performance certainly enter the equation, but only after the initial facts have been established. When evaluating paraeducator performance it is sometimes helpful to use a rubric based on level of independent performance of the task. Table 9.1 contains a rubric that may be applied to paraeducator performance and may be used in conjunction with the personalized job description, rating each assigned task. Or the rubric may be used as an add-on to the district-required evaluation form for classified employees.

Table 9.1   Rubric for Judging Level of Task Independence

Assigned Task (Taken from personalized job description)	Level of Independence				
	Independent[a]	Developing[b]	Emerging[c]	Unable[d]	Unwilling[e]

a. Paraeducator is able to perform task, as taught, without guidance.
b. Paraeducator can perform task, as taught, but relies on cues or prompts for portions of the performance.
c. Paraeducator performs parts of task or tries to perform but requires substantial guidance to complete all aspects.
d. Paraeducator does not know how to perform the task.
e. Paraeducator is unwilling to perform the task.

CHAPTER SUMMARY

When orientation, planning, scheduling, training, delegation, and direction are already in place, monitoring the work of paraeducators is the next step. Teachers have not had this responsibility in the past, and some teachers will not see this as a legitimate part of their responsibilities. Administrators who want to encourage teachers to grow as team leaders may coach them in the skills of monitoring and begin to require teachers to be accountable for the outcomes of the work of the entire team—including paraeducators. Performance monitoring requires observations and those may be focused or unfocused, but either way they should be frequent and short. Teachers may provide formative feedback to paraeducators, but summative evaluation remains within the role of administrators. The data collected by teachers and shared with paraeducators should inform the final summative evaluation conducted by the administrator.

10 Managing the Workplace

Managing the workplace is the final, but by no means the least, of the executive functions of paraeducator supervision. Teachers, nurses, library and media specialists, occupational therapists, school psychologists, and speech-language specialists—all the professionals that comprise our educational system—need to begin to think of themselves as executives and as team leaders. When paraeducators work in the school, they automatically become a part of several teams with different structures. For example, the health room assistant is a part of the district-level health team, probably led by a nurse who is assigned to multiple school buildings, but provides direction and supervision regarding student health needs. The health room assistant is also part of the front office team in the building and probably receives some daily direction on those responsibilities from the principal or assistant principal. Of course, this association with multiple teams means that there is an ongoing need for effective and efficient communications, problem solving, and conflict management.

McKinley Elementary School, featured in Chapter 1, is an example of a smoothly functioning school in which 21 paraeducators work. They perform many different jobs within the school and have very different schedules and responsibilities. They come from different cultures and have different styles, linguistic backgrounds, and aspirations. There is plenty of opportunity for conflict and disputes do arise periodically. Sometimes the dissent is between two or more paraeducators, and sometimes it is between a paraeducator and a professional from a different program. Each paraeducator is a member of a program within the school, and therefore a member of the program team. Some teams are very small (two people) and some are very loosely coupled, to be sure. Yet, each team is similar in that there is a professional at the head of the team. Even in the library, where Joye helps students find research materials and books to read, the team consists of a professional library and media specialist who supervises Joye as well as eight other elementary library assistants across the district. Joye's supervisor and team leader is only in the building once every two weeks, so Joye operates quite independently most of the time. When the supervisor is in the building, they spend their time together considering the various problematic situations and think together how to handle them. They communicate about goals, plans, and schedules. The library and media specialist gives Joye feedback on her performance and coaches her on essential tasks. When conflicts arise between Joye and other paraeducators or teachers in the building, the library and media professional sometimes steps in to help.

Similarly, Rae and Tami are members of a team led by the speech-language specialist and they travel together with the speech-language specialist, Tracy, to three different schools delivering services each day. Rae and Tami work in the same building with Tracy every day, but the nature of their job requires that they enter and leave half a dozen classrooms a day. Each classroom is led by a teacher with unique preferences and needs and they have little time to communicate about them. Yet, the need for communications is great and the opportunities for problems and conflict are many. Therefore, Tracy spends time consulting and communicating with teachers, solving various logistical and instructional problems, and intervenes when conflicts arise. Because it takes time to collaborate in this way with classroom teachers, Rae and Tami are often providing direct services to students while Tracy is engaged with teachers for planning and problem solving.

Effective communication, problem solving, and conflict management among professionals and between professionals and paraeducators are essential. Together, they are the processes that comprise the executive function referred to as *workplace management*. School professionals must plan to accomplish each workplace management component. The first plan should address the development and maintenance of effective communication systems. The second plan should develop and sustain a problem-solving sequence that can be employed whenever student, logistical, or instructional problems are not easily resolved. The third plan addresses workplace conflict and recognizes the importance of team leadership in resolving or managing it.

ESTABLISHING AND MAINTAINING EFFECTIVE COMMUNICATIONS

Communication is the most fundamental of all team skills. Effective communication requires skill, but even highly skilled team members cannot consistently share information if there is no system. Yet, team leaders sometimes forget to establish systems by which the very best communication can occur.

Communication Systems

The best communication systems allow for two-way communication. Often they are based on student needs, individualized plans, or lesson or activity plans. Communication systems should be built into plans. The plan forms shown in Chapter 7 all provide information to paraeducators about the supports and instruction they need to provide to students and all include systems by which paraeducators can feed information back to the professional(s) who created the plan. Of course, written forms are just one type of communication system.

Other communication systems that are used quite successfully by teachers everywhere include numerous asynchronous methods such as back-and-forth books, sticky notes, notes on bulletin boards, e-mail messages, and voice messages. Teams develop routine spots where they can leave notes they know will be read. They plan their communications. In some schools where instant communication is important, paraeducators carry walkie-talkies or cell phones when working in distant parts of the building or campus. No matter how good a team is at communicating via written plans or other asynchronous means or even by walkie-talkie, sometimes face-to-face communications are necessary. Face-to-face communications generally mean meetings.

Meetings

It's difficult to find a teacher who likes meetings. For many teachers, meetings mean wasting time. Teachers say that they go to too many meetings, spend too much time in meetings, and get too little done in meetings. Too often, teachers have experienced meetings that are entirely didactic, with someone lecturing or reading information. They realize that the same information could be presented in written form, via fliers in mailboxes or via e-mail. They have experienced meetings where one individual does all the talking, taking up valuable time on a single issue. Sometimes groups spend too much time hashing over the same issues time and again, with the same results.

Other teachers have fewer negative feelings about meetings and when asked why that is so, they report experiences with meetings that are productive because problems are solved, genuine communication occurs among colleagues, or conflicts are resolved. When teachers experience productive meetings in which they play an active part—thinking and working—and where the results are implemented, they actually like them.

Whether teachers like meetings or not, in teams that include paraeducators, regularly scheduled meetings are a necessary part of communication, problem solving, and conflict management. There are six considerations for planning to have regularly scheduled, productive meetings with paraeducators: time, group norms, meeting location, agendas, documenting decisions, and reviewing effectiveness of meetings.

Time

Finding time to hold meetings is problematic. Paraeducators often work the same hours that students attend school, and in many places are not paid for any time beyond the student attendance hours. Several solutions can be considered. One option is to pay paraeducators to attend team meetings. Paying paraeducators for their time beyond student attendance hours is good practice. It means that meetings can be held when there are no students around and fewer distractions, in general. Meetings that are effectively planned and led require only about 45 minutes per week.

At the pay rate of $10.00 per hour, the cost to the district would be about $300 per year—a relatively small price to pay for improved team effectiveness. If that isn't possible, a second option involves the use of flex-time. Flex-time is different from comp time and doesn't involve any overtime or additional pay. To clarify the difference, consider that comp time essentially says to the para-educator, "Work extra hours now and you can have time off sometime in the undefined future." While this practice is employed in some places, and sometimes accomplishes the goal of having meeting time, it is illegal. Fair labor laws protect workers from this type of potential abuse. In addition, the liability issues involved are significant. If a paraeducator were hurt or involved in any kind of incident at school outside her assigned work hours, the school district would require legal counsel to determine the liability involved. In other words, making deals with paraeducators to work extra hours or to take unscheduled time off is a practice that is both illegal and unwise.

Flex-time is legal and means that, on a preplanned and regularly scheduled basis, the paraeducator's schedule includes a late start or early finish time one day per week. To balance out the schedule, neither adding nor subtracting any hours from the weekly schedule, one day per week is extended to allow for before or after school meeting time. The late start or early finish may or may not be on the same day as the meeting.

Group Norms

Once the "when" question is resolved, the next issue is to establish group norms. A group norm is anything that the team establishes that is an agreed-upon policy. Group norms include meeting facilitation, meeting procedures, how decisions are made, or style of meeting. Sometimes a team decides to have refreshments at meetings and agrees to spend time making a schedule for who brings the food or beverage. Other teams find refreshments too time-consuming and distracting. Some teams start the meeting with kudos or recognition of special events in the lives of team members. Others start with the business at hand and leave personal issues outside the meeting. Group norms take many forms, and no particular form is preferable. The group has to live with the norms they make and should create those with which they are comfortable.

Location. The most effective meetings occur away from distractions and where students or school visitors are not likely to overhear conversations about confidential matters. A closed door improves the productivity of the team and the efficiency of the meeting.

Facilitation. The person who leads or coordinates the meeting may be obvious in some teams, but in others may be decided by the team. Sometimes teachers who have participated in effective meetings find themselves able to use the techniques they've witnessed in their meetings with paraeducators. They've learned some good meeting facilitation techniques by osmosis.

More often, teachers have had little experience with effective meeting leadership and have had little training on meeting facilitation. These teachers need to develop specific meeting management skills to be effective with para-

Table 10.1   Effective Meeting Resources

Books

Bradford, L. P. (1976). *Making meetings work: A guide for leaders and group members.* San Diego, CA: University Associates.

Doyle, M., & Straus, D. (1976). *How to make meetings work.* New York: Jove Books.

Kelsey, D., and Plumb, P. (1997). *Great meetings! How to facilitate like a pro.* Maine: Hanson Park Press.

Tropman, J. E. (1980). *Effective meetings: Improving group decision–making.* Beverly Hills, CA: Sage.

Web Sites

McNamara, C. (1991). *Basic guide to conducting effective meetings.* Retrieved from: www.mapnp.org/library/misc/mtgmgmnt.htm

Meeting Planning Center, Meeting Wizard.com Retrieved from: www.meetingwizard.org/meetings/3_0.cfm

U.S. Department of Justice, Youth in Action Newsletter (1999, September, Number 10). Retrieved from: www.ncjrs.org/pdffiles1/ojjdp/171692.pdf

educators. There are many resources available for teachers who want to improve meeting facilitation skills. Several currently available sources are included in Table 10.1.

Reviewing Meeting Effectiveness. Team members should take time periodically, to ask themselves how their team is functioning and how their meetings are working.

Set formats are not necessary. Honest conversations that begin with the question, "Are we accomplishing our goals in our meetings?" are necessary.

Agendas

The use of an agenda is the first step to holding an effective meeting. Too often, team meetings degenerate into complaint sessions where a problematic student is discussed or school politics are bantered about. Sometimes complaints merge into gossip about families of students, other faculty, or absent team members. To avoid all these time-wasting and possibly destructive conversations, an agenda should be developed and used.

The process of developing the agenda. Agendas may be developed in several ways. The meeting facilitator may develop the agenda using his or her own memories to include items that seem to be of the greatest concern to team members. Better yet, the facilitator can provide the format for the agenda, and perhaps some of the items, but leave the form or format in a public place so that others can add items that need to be addressed in a meeting. For example, an electronic form can be placed on the school's computer network where everyone can access it. Then, on meeting day, someone just presses the print button to have a prepared agenda. Other, low-tech options include placing a form on a bulletin board or in a folder on a shared table or desk. Team members add items when they think of them. If there are too many items on the agenda to address in a single meeting, the team leader or the group must prioritize the items to address immediately and those to hold for another day. When an agenda is not preplanned, it can be developed during the first few minutes of the meeting. This technique works well in well-established and high-functioning teams where no one is disruptive or overly aggressive. Table 10.2 contains a sample form that may be used as a template for developing a functional agenda.

The content of the agenda. Agendas give focus to the meeting and to the team members. They can allow limited time for personal conversations, sharing of experiences, or catch-up on the lives of all the team members. However, the primary purpose is to ensure that the team is communicating well and that everyone has vital information. Agendas ensure that problems that must be addressed are brought to the group for deliberation. Agendas can help manage conflict by bringing the interpersonal issues into the open and allowing the time to address them. Notice that the agenda form in Table 10.2 includes spaces in which to identify who will facilitate the meeting, who will take notes, and

Table 10.2   Agenda Form

AGENDA	
Date: **Time:**	
Facilitator:	
Note taker:	
Timekeeper:	
Attendees:	
Please read:	
Please bring:	
Agenda Items	
	Time Allotment
1. 2. 3. 4. 5. 6. 7. 8.	

who will keep time. It also has a place to list who attended the meeting and what participants need to read, bring, or think about ahead of time. Each agenda item also has a place next to it in which to put the time allotment for that item.

Following the agenda. Even the best-written agenda is useless if it is not followed. The team leader generally leads the meeting and manages the agenda, ensuring that adequate time is allowed for each item and that no item is allowed to take the entire meeting time. Sometimes team leaders ask other team members to play leadership roles as well. For example, Sue is known for her impatience with long conversations. Sue may be asked to be the timekeeper and may be given public permission to interrupt conversations that extend past the allotted time by saying, "We've used the allotted time for this topic. Do we want to continue and exclude something else on the agenda, or do we need to stop now and revisit the topic at another meeting?" Having clearly established group norms ahead of time makes this possible.

Documenting Decisions

One of the most frustrating aspects of meetings is discussing the same topic again because no decision was made or because the decisions that were made were not recorded. Memory is not to be trusted. Individuals tend to remember events differently. However, taking minutes of the meeting in a traditional way is not necessary. Minutes of meetings often contain a lot of detail about all the conversation and are usually taken by someone who is serving as secretary to the meeting rather than by a meeting participant. Team meetings generally cannot afford this luxury. So, to make the most effective use of precious meeting time, have a participant briefly record decisions and check them with the group during the meeting. This habit is well-rewarded. Subsequent agendas can include the follow-up steps or consist of progress reports on items. Table 10.3 contains a form that may be used as a template for decisions and meeting notes.

PROBLEM SOLVING

Sometimes paraeducators and professionals need to jointly solve problems that have to do with students, schedules, materials use, space, and instruction. This can be done most efficiently and effectively when team members agree on a problem-solving process.

Teams that use the process frequently minimize the time it takes to complete the process, but even the most experienced teams admit it requires sustained effort.

Recognize the Existence of and Define the Problem

Many individuals want to ignore this step because they assume that everyone sees the problem in precisely the same way that they do. In most groups of people, nothing could be further from the truth. Rarely do two people see a sit-

Table 10.3   Decisions Form

DECISIONS	Date Time		
Note taker:			
Discussion:			
Conclusions:			
Action items		**Person responsible**	**Deadline**

uation exactly the same way. Making early assumptions about the nature of the problem can lead to grave errors later on in the process.

Problems that are stated in terms of competing solutions make it difficult to get to the heart of the issue. At the core of every effective solution is a productively defined problem. Haphazard application of solutions and misplaced solutions, at best, waste our time and frustrate our students. In the worst cases, poor solutions do significant damage to our students.

Decide Whether to Solve the Problem

Not every problem needs to be solved—or, indeed, can be solved. If the group sees the problem as outside its control, there is no point in trying. The team may choose at this point to redefine the problem as something that can be addressed by school personnel and then to continue through the problem-solving process, or it may decide to live with the conflict or dilemma as it is.

Decide the Criteria for a Successful Solution

Deciding the criteria for a successful solution is the step that considers the outcomes the team wants. Criteria by which solutions are to be considered become most important in teams where members have different values or purposes. Yet, this step is often neglected. Deciding what constitutes a good solution saves time implementing solutions that no one can support or that may have unintended side effects. Criteria are inevitably value-based. Negotiating agreement among people who hold conflicting values is a difficult and time-consuming business, but it is critically important.

Generate Possible Alternative Solutions

There are numerous methods by which to generate possible alternative solutions. The most familiar (but not necessarily the most effectively used) method is brainstorming. This process requires group members to call out ideas as they think of them, facilitating their own thinking by listening to and building on the ideas generated by other group members. Effective brainstorming occurs when all ideas that are offered are initially accepted and when there are lots of different possibilities generated. Usually, all the ideas are written down, without editing, for all to see.

Although there is obviously a point of diminishing returns, a greater volume of ideas and proposals generally leads to a higher-quality decision. The adventurousness of participants tends to be compromised by premature evaluation of ideas, so brainstorming processes are predicated on the initial acceptance of all ideas.

Compare Each Alternative to the Criteria

At this stage, the team applies the criteria to the list of ideas they have generated, choosing the solution that seems to best fit the outcomes they are trying to achieve, with the fewest side effects.

Select One or More Alternatives to Implement

In this phase of the process the team decides among alternatives that remain after they discard those that don't meet the criteria. Often, there are more ideas that can be reasonably implemented, so teams have to apply common sense in choosing those that are the easiest and those that are, in their opinions, most likely to succeed.

Plan How to Monitor and Evaluate the Solution

The final step in the problem-solving process is to decide how to determine whether the solutions work. Team members must agree what information will prove the solution worked.

DEALING WELL WITH DIFFERENCES

When adults work together, it is inevitable that conflict will arise. The presence of conflict does not mean that the team members are bad people. It just means that there are differences in their ways of thinking about and doing things. Failing to deal well with differences, however, can disrupt the work of the team and may prevent effective teaching and learning.

Sometimes teachers and related service providers who have not yet begun to think of themselves as executives or as team leaders fail to understand conflict as one of the workplace management functions. They may not have developed skills to handle the related responsibilities. Like some administrators, they expect that good people will always see eye to eye. In real life, even good, highly committed people have differences. The ability of the adults to deal well with their differences is the feature that makes McKinley Elementary run smoothly.

Sources of School Conflict

There are six typical sources of school conflict: relationships, data or information, values, structural issues, interests, and personal preferences and styles. Figure 10.1 shows the circle of conflict in which three of the causes are in the top half and three are in the bottom half of the circle. When a conflict arises it is helpful to identify the source of the conflict because the source may help determine the course of action. The first three causes, in the bottom half of the circle, are the most easily resolved conflicts. However, there are no guarantees. If you put substantial effort into resolving a conflict, and it remains unresolved, you may give up trying to resolve it and decide simply to manage the differences. The three sources in the top half of the circle are more likely to be irresolvable, and therefore efforts should be directed toward management.

Personal Styles and Preferences

Personal styles and preferences are neither inherently right nor inherently wrong. However, differences in style may cause irritation and sometimes open conflict. While individuals are what they are and are unlikely to change preferences or styles, they can adapt, adjust, or flex a little so that positive working relationships are possible. The tables provided in Chapter 5, if used early in the working relationship, can help teams avoid conflicts about personal styles or preferences. In situations where the conflict has already developed, the tables may be used to get to the heart of the issues and help all the parties to the conflict determine what adjustments are necessary.

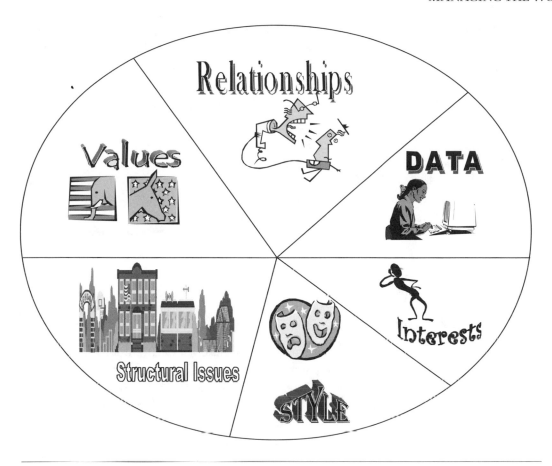

Figure 10.1. Circle of Conflict

Structural Issues

Conflicts that arise because of structural issues are also resolvable. Such conflicts tend to be about roles and responsibilities, time, schedules, resources, or space. Disputes over such structural issues can be addressed and unfair situations rectified.

Interests

Conflicts that involve different interests can also be resolved in many cases. Interest-based conflicts may involve perceived differences in status, power, respect, control, or recognition. Or the interests may be substantive differences in the amount or quality of resources or materials. Procedural issues may also become the source of conflict. The way that decisions are made, who is included in the decision, who has a voice in the process, and the steps taken to reach a goal may be of great concern to team members.

Relationships

If the conflict stems from a history of poor relationships, strong emotions, misperceptions, stereotypes, poor communication, or negative repetitive behaviors, the conflict may not be resolvable. Long-seated anger or hostility feeds on itself and grows beyond normal proportions. In the workplace, two individuals who dislike one another intensely may have to work together, but nothing will force them to like one another. Attempts to resolve such a conflict could be time-consuming and are unlikely to be productive. Such conflicts can be managed effectively, even though they may never achieve resolution.

Values

When the conflict is based on core values held by the participants in the conflict, there may be no way to resolve it. Values derive from long-held convictions, religious or familial teaching, or other belief syems, but are not necessarily based in reason or logic. If a conflict involves a significant difference in values, it is not probable that you, or anyone else, will be able to convince either party to change. Similarly, value-based conflicts may be managed but probably cannot be resolved.

Information

Different data—that is, information or different interpretations of the same information—are another source of conflict. Two people can view the same event and describe it differently. They may read the same statistics and derive different conclusions. They may hear the same words and read the communicative intent differently. Underlying attitudes, emotions, or beliefs form a lens through which a person views everything. There is little you can do in the workplace to change that lens.

Resolving Conflict

If the problem has been acknowledged, resolution seems possible, the cause of the conflict is in the bottom half of the circle (personal styles, interests, or structural issues), and the parties are willing to devote the time it takes, then the following steps will help.

First, gain agreement among all parties to resolve the conflict. This isn't necessarily easy to do. Sometimes a person who is outside the circle of this particular conflict may act as mediator. Consider the motivations of the parties in the conflict. Sometimes an individual fails to understand that it is in his or her best interest to resolve the dispute. Do the parties understand why it would be in their best interest to resolve the conflict? Is the conflict having negative effects on the parties or is it possible that one of the parties is gaining a positive effect from the conflict? Consider what will happen if the conflict goes on without intervention. Identify the interests of each party and consider what each needs to get out of it in the end.

Second, clarify what the conflict is about. Parties in conflict may believe they know the cause of the conflict, but their initial diagnosis may be in error. Conflicts perceived to be rooted in actions or behaviors are often about communication failures, interests, or structural issues. By the time conflict reaches a level where people are willing to deal with it, the real conflict is actually an accumulation of half-remembered events or circumstances. The act of clarifying the basis of the conflict often helps the individuals see that there were a lot of hurt feelings, but little substance. If this is the case, the following steps will go very quickly. Deliberate workplace attempts to harm another person are extremely rare. More often, someone has been inconsiderate of or oblivious to the needs of others.

The third step is to generate a variety of options that would restore equitable schedules, responsibilities, use of time or resources, a balance of interests, or a mesh of personal styles. This step is only possible when the conflict is about the issues in the lower half of the circle. For value-, relationship-, or information-based conflicts, it is unlikely that anyone could find options that would truly resolve the conflict. After the options have been generated, consider which options meet all the identified needs. If none of the options meet the criteria, return to the third step and generate other ideas.

The fourth step is to select a solution and gain agreement from both parties to adhere to the selected solution. If either party is hesitant, unable, or unwilling to stick to the agreed-upon solution, go back to the drawing board. An unused solution is no better than no solution at all.

Fifth, to be certain that you have created a solution that will work, make up an implementation plan specifying who does what, where, when, and how. Work through some hypothetical, but probable, situations with the parties to be sure that each party knows what they must do in the situation. You will know that you have resolved or settled the conflict when it no longer consumes energy of the group or of individual team members.

Managing Conflict

Often, the best we can do in a conflict that stems from issues in the top half of the circle of conflict (relationships, values, and data) is manage it. Sometimes the causes of those conflicts run so deep or are so rooted in the individual that the workplace is not the venue in which to attempt resolution. The effective team leader will live by the motto "Let me resolve the conflicts that I can, manage those I can't, and be wise enough to know the difference."

In conflict management, like conflict resolution, there is a series of steps. The first step is to identify the cause of the conflict. Once the conflict is identified or assessed, the second step is to acknowledge some of the most serious aspects or side effects of the conflict. The third step is to publicly acknowledge that the goal is to manage the conflict. Conflict management means that you intend to minimize the negative effects of the conflict, while recognizing that you have done nothing to resolve the basis of the conflict itself. The fourth step is to generate various options and to consider the implications of each. When the team considers the implications, they ask themselves questions about what effect the conflict is having on their ability to work effectively as a team, about what effects it has on others in the school, and about the effect it has on themselves. For example, some questions that address the effects on others include, "What will students see if we do this?" and "What will parents and community members see if we do this?" and "What will other school employees see if we do this?"

Skills for Conflict Resolution and Conflict Management

The success of conflict resolution and conflict management lies in the skills of the parties in conflict. Good communication skills, such as good listening habits, phrasing of caring confrontation statements, and the ability to positively reframe and restate problems in less inflammatory words, increase the likelihood of achieving a resolution. If no resolution is likely, those same skills contribute to effective conflict management.

Communication skills can be taught and learned. If parties to conflict are unable to listen carefully, there are exercises that can help. However, such skills are best learned outside of the circle of conflict in a neutral classroom or workshop situation.

Learning to restate problems positively is also a skill worth learning. Some parties to conflict restate issues using more inflammatory language or put a negative spin on the words of the other party. Putting a positive spin on words is only possible if there is genuine intent to resolve the conflict along with skills. The outside person can ask the parties involved in the conflict to do three things to enhance conflict management.

First, ask those who disagree to paraphrase one another's comments. This may help the parties come to understand the other person's point of view. Second, have each side write 10 questions for the person with whom they have the conflict. This will allow each side to signal their major concerns about the other position. The answers can sometimes lead to a compromise solution. Finally, ask each party to list what they want the other party to do. Exchange lists, and together select those that all can agree to.

CHAPTER SUMMARY

Well-functioning workplaces are based on effective teamwork. Many effective teams have team leaders, and in schools the team leader manages the workplace. Team leaders establish systems for communicating, solving problems, and managing or resolving conflicts.

Final Thoughts for School Administrators and Teachers Who Supervise Paraeducators

While most administrators know and treasure the individuals who work in their schools, the work of paraeducators in our public education system has remained largely unnoticed by the general public. There is no Channel 6 "Paraeducator Who Cares" Award and no advertisements on TV saying "Be a paraeducator—be a hero!" Paraeducators are not featured on the cover of a journal called "Paraeducation Today." The fact is their work is rarely featured in mainstream literature on educational practice. Books and articles on teaching routinely ignore the paraeducator role in instruction, behavior support, student support, and curricular adaptation. Articles and books on how students learn are not aimed at an audience of paraeducators. In fact, there is no journal or magazine that targets this important group of educational personnel.

Nor is it much mentioned in the literature that, like teachers, paraeducators require effective supervision to perform their best. There is no specific mention of paraeducator supervision in preparation programs for school administrators. So, new administrators are not prepared to support teachers who find themselves in an unexpected role. Few articles about supervising paraeducators appear in administrators' journals. Supervisory skills are not systematically taught to preservice teachers, nurses, or school psychologists. Programs that prepare speech-language pathologists, physical therapists, and occupational therapists sometimes touch on the subject, but generally couch it in clinical or hospital settings rather than education. While some articles have appeared in teacher-practitioner journals that address teachers and their work with paraeducators, teachers are not at liberty to take on a strong supervisory role without the support, cooperation, and guidance of the building administrator.

In recent years, there has been a growing controversy over the employment of paraeducators. While advocates believe that the employment of paraeducators offers tremendous opportunities to educators and the U.S. educational system, critics oppose the use of paraeducators in schools. Potentially, a teacher paired with a paraeducator can reach twice as many students and provide more caring, consistent, high-quality education. Yet, the dual problems of poor training and supervision have undermined this powerful potential. Critics are concerned that we are providing poorer quality education to children who are already at risk for school failure because we employ poorly trained and poorly supervised paraeducators.

So, if you are a school administrator or a teacher, you may want to keep this book on top of your desk. Use it as a handy reference to help decide how to staff your special education or Title I program—within budget. Or pick it up when you are considering whether hiring a paraeducator to serve a special education student is the right decision. Or pull out the library-media table to decide how to staff your library. Consider the pros and cons of staffing your health room by employing a nurse or a paraeducator. When you are ready to advertise and hire a highly qualified paraeducator, pull out the checklists to be sure you have tapped all sources. Plan to start new paraeducators off on the right foot by using the introductions checklist as a guide. Use the tables in Chapter 5 to help clarify roles, so everyone knows who does what. Use Table 8.2 to decide how to select the right training material for paraeducators on a limited budget. If you want to base your staff evaluations on data and to ensure that teachers and paraeducators work together as a team, then this book is for you.

Suggested Reading

Allington, R. L., & Cunningham, P. M. (1996). *Schools that work: Where all children read and write*. New York: HarperCollins College.

American Federation of Teachers. (1997). Non-nursing school personnel. In *The medically fragile child in the school setting* (2nd ed., Chap. 4, pp. 33-36). Washington, DC: Author.

American Federation of Teachers. (1999, September). Saving Title I. *Paraprofessional and School-Related Personnel Reporter, 1*, 6-7.

American Speech-Language-Hearing Association. (1995). *Guidelines for the training, credentializing, use and supervision of speech-language pathology assistants*. Rockville, MD: Author.

Berliner, D. (1983a). The executive functions of teaching. *Instructor, 93*(2), 28-33, 36, 38, 40.

Berliner, D. C. (1983b). *If teachers were thought of as executives: Implications for teacher preparation and certification*. Paper prepared for the National Institute of Education Conference on State and Local Policy Implications of Effective School Research. (EDRS Document No. 245357)

Boyd-Zaharias, J., & Pate-Bain, H. (1998). *Teacher aides and student learning: Lessons from Project STAR*. Arlington, VA: Educational Research Service.

Brown, L., Farrington, K., Knight, T., Ross, C., & Ziegler, M. (1999). Fewer paraeducators and more teachers and therapists in educational programs for students with significant disabilities. *Journal of the Association for Persons with Severe Handicaps, 24*(4), 250-253.

Cooper, M. P., & Cobb, H. Jr. (1983). *Assessment of services provided by paraeducators*. Washington, DC: District of Columbia Public Schools.

Coots, J. J., Bishop, K. D., & Grenot-Scheyer, M. (1998). Supporting elementary age students with significant disabilities in general education classrooms: Personal perspectives on inclusion. *Education and Training in Mental Retardation and Developmental Disabilities, 33*(4), 317-330.

Coufal, K. L., Steckelberg, A. L., & Vasa, S. F. (1991). Current trends in the training and utilization of paraeducators in speech and language programs: A report on an eleven-state survey. *Language, Speech, and Hearing Services in Schools, 22*, 51-59.

Courson, F. H., & Heward, W. L. (1988). Increasing active student response through the effective use of paraprofessionals. *The Pointer, 33*(1), 27-31.

Covey, S. R. (1989). *The 7 habits of highly successful people*. New York: Simon & Schuster.

Darling-Hammond, L. (1990). Teachers and teaching: Signs of a changing profession. In W. R. Houston, M. Haberman, & J. Sikula (Eds.), *Handbook of research on teacher education* (pp. 267-290). New York: Macmillan.

Downing, J. E., Ryndak, D. L., & Clark, D. (2000). Paraeducators in inclusive classrooms: Their own perceptions. *Remedial and Special Education, 21*(3), 171-181.

Emery, M. J. (1991). *Building team pride: Teachers and paraeducators working together.* Columbus: University of Missouri.

Fisher, D., Sax, C., Rodifer, K., & Pumpian, I. (1999). Teachers' perspectives of curriculum and climate changes. *Journal for a Just and Caring Education, 5*(3), 256-268.

French, N. K. (1991). Elementary teachers' perceptions of stressful events and stress related teaching practices. *Perceptual and Motor Skills, 72,* 203-210.

French, N. K. (1993). The relationship of class size to perceived teacher stress. *Journal of Research and Development in Education, 26*(2), 66-73.

French, N. K. (1996). A case study of a speech-language pathologist's supervision of assistants in a school setting: Tracy's story. *Journal for Children's Communication Development, 18*(1), 103-110.

French, N. K. (1997). Management of paraeducators. In A. L. Pickett & K. Gerlach (Eds.), *Working with paraeducators in special education: A team approach* (pp. 91-169). Austin, TX: Pro-ed.

French, N. K. (1998). Working together: Resource teachers and paraeducators. *Remedial and Special Education, 19*(6), 357-368.

French, N. K. (2001). Supervising paraprofessionals: A survey of teacher practices. *Journal of Special Education, 35*(1), 41-53.

French, N. K. (2002). Managing paraeducators. In A. L. Pickett & K. Gerlach (Eds.), *Supervising paraeducators in school settings: A team approach* (2nd ed.). Austin, TX: Pro-ed.

French, N. K., Beckman, V., Berg de Balderas, H., Chopra, R. V., Friedman, K., Stimson, B., & Pickett, A. L. (2002). *Paraeducator duties, training considerations, and career development possibilities.* Manuscript in preparation.

French, N. K., & Chopra, R. V. (1999). Parent perspectives on the role of the paraprofessional in inclusion. *Journal of the Association for Persons with Severe Handicaps, 24*(4), 259-272.

French, N. K., & Gerlach, K. P. (1998, February). *What does it mean to be a professional educator? Role differentiation for paraprofessionals and professionals.* Paper presented at the American Association of Colleges of Teacher Education Annual Meeting, New Orleans, LA.

French, N. K., & Lee, P. (1988). *Guidelines for effective utilization of paraprofessionals in special education.* Denver: Colorado Department of Education.

French, N. K., & Pickett, A. L. (1997). Paraprofessionals in special education: Issues for teacher educators. *Teacher Education and Special Education, 20*(1), 61-73.

Freschi, D. F. (1999). Guidelines for working with one-to-one aides. *Teaching Exceptional Children, 31*(4), 42-45.

Fryer, G. E., Jr., & Igoe, J. B. (1996). Functions of school nurses and health assistants in U.S. school health programs. *Journal of School Health, 66*(2), 55-58.

Gartner, A. (1971). *Paraeducators and their performance: A survey of education, health and social services programs.* New York: Praeger.

Genzuk, M., Lavadenz, M., & Krashen, S. (1994). Paraeducators: A source for remedying the shortage of teachers for limited-English-proficient students. *Journal of Educational Issues of Language Minority Students, 14,* 211-222.

Giangreco, M. F., Edelman, S. W., Luiselli, T. E., & MacFarland, S. Z. C. (1997). Helping or hovering? Effects of instructional assistant proximity on students with disabilities. *Exceptional Children, 64,* 7-18.

Glass, G. V., & Smith, M. L. (1978). *Meta-analysis of research on the relationship of class size and achievement* (No. OB-NIE-G-78-0103). San Francisco: Far West Laboratory for Educational Research and Development.

Guess, D., Smith, J. O., & Ensminger, E. E. (1971). The role of nonprofessional persons in teaching language skills to mentally retarded children. *Exceptional Children, 37,* 447-453.

Hansen, D. (1996). Use of focus-group needs assessment for planning paraprofessional staff development in Iowa's education settings. *Journal of Children's Communication Development, 18*(1), 81-90.

Heller, W. (1997). Professional and ethical responsibilities of team members. In A. L. Pickett & K. Gerlach (Eds.), *Working with paraeducators in special education: A team approach* (pp. 207-234). Austin, TX: Pro-ed.

Individuals with Disabilities Education Act of 1997, 20 U.S.C. § 1401.

Innocenti, M. (1993). Paraeducators in early intervention: Some information and some ideas. *New Directions, 14*(4), 1, 3.

Innocenti, M. S., & Roberts, R. N. (1995, May). *Using paraeducators to provide early intervention services: Lessons learned and useful directions.* Paper presented at the Contemporary Trends in Special Education Conference, Pedagogical University, Krakow, Poland.

Johnson, L. (1994, Fall). Setting standards: A certification process will help ensure that education paraeducators are well prepared to work with students. *Paraprofessional and School-Related Personnel Reporter,* 1-4.

Joyce, B., & Showers, B. (1980). Improving inservice training: The messages of research. *Educational Leadership, 37,* 379-385.

Katsiyannis, A., Hodge, J., & Lanford, A. (2000). Paraeducators: Legal and practice considerations. *Remedial and Special Education, 21*(5), 297-304.

Katsiyannis, A., & Yell, M. L. (2000). The Supreme Court and school health services: Cedar Rapids v. Garret F. *Exceptional Children, 66*(3), 317-326.

Kotkin, R. (1998). The Irvine paraeducator program: Promising practice for serving students with ADHD. *Journal of Learning Disabilities, 31*(6), 556-564.

LeTendre, M. J. (n.d.). *Paraprofessionals: A resource for tomorrow's teachers.* Retrieved January 22, 1999 from U.S. Department of Education Web site: http://www.ed.gov/compensatory_education_programs

Lindeman, D. P., & Beegle, G. B. (1988). Preservice teacher training and use of the classroom paraprofessional: A national survey. *Teacher Education and Special Education, 11,* 184-186.

Marks, S. U., Schrader, C., & Levine, M. (1999). Paraeducator experiences in inclusive settings: Helping, hovering, or holding their own? *Exceptional Children, 65*(3), 315-328.

May, D. C., & Marozas, D. S. (1986). Working with paraprofessionals: Are teachers of persons with severe handicapping conditions being prepared for this responsibility? *DPH Journal, 9,* 22-26.

McIntyre, N. D. (1999). *It does make a difference: Teacher aide support for secondary school students.* Unpublished thesis, Massey University, Albany, New Zealand.

Miller, M. D., Brownell, M. T., & Smith, S. W. (1999). Factors that predict teachers staying in, leaving, or transferring from the special education classroom. *Exceptional Children, 65*(2), 201-218.

Miramontes, O. B., Nadeau, A., & Commins, N. L. (1997). *Restructuring Schools for Linguistic Diversity.* New York: Teacher's College Press.

Morgan, B. (1997). *The S___ word: What teachers consider important in the supervision of paraeducators.* Paper presented at the 16th Annual Conference on the Training and Employment of the Paraprofessional Workforce in Education, Rehabilitation, and Related Fields, Los Angeles, CA.

Phillips, S., & Krajicek, M. J. (1994, August). Delegation: Invasive procedures—children with disabilities. In M. J. Krajicek (Ed.), *Meeting the challenge of inclusion for young children with special health care needs.* Denver, CO: National Conference on Developing Policy and Practice to Implement IDEA Related to Invasive Procedures for Children with Special Health Care Needs.

Pickett, A. L. (1986). Certified partners: Four good reasons for certification of para-educators. *American Educator, 10*(3), 31-34, 47.

Pickett, A. L. (1994). *Paraeducators in the education workforce.* Washington, DC: National Education Association.

Radaszewski-Byrne, M. (1996). Issues in the development of guidelines for the preparation and use of speech-language paraeducators and their SL supervisors working in education settings. *Journal of Children's Communication Development, 18*(1), 5-22.

Rapport, M. J. K. (1996). Legal guidelines for the delivery of special health care services in school. *Exceptional Children, 62,* 537-549.

Reid, B., & Johnston, M. (1978). Paraprofessionals in education for the severely / profoundly handicapped. In N. G. Haring & D. D. Bricker (Eds.), *Teaching the severely handicapped* (pp. 77-93). Columbus, OH: Special Press.

Rubin, P. M. (1994). *Who is teaching our children: A look at the use of aides in Chapter 1.* Washington, DC: International Reading Association.

Rubin, P. M., & Long, R. M. (1994, Spring). Who is teaching our children: Implications of the use of aides in Chapter 1. *ERS Spectrum,* 28-34.

Salisbury, C. L., Evans, I. M., & Paombaro, M. M. (1997). Collaborative problem-solving to promote the inclusion of young children with significant disabilities in primary grades. *Exceptional Children, 63*(2), 195-209.

Salzberg, C. L., & Morgan, J. (1995). Preparing teachers to work with paraeducators. *Teacher Education and Special Education, 18*(1), 49-55.

Schortinguis, N. E., & Frohman, A. (1974). A comparison of paraeducator and professional success with preschool children. *Journal of Learning Disabilities, 7*(4), 245-247.

Shearer, M. S., & Shearer, D. E. (1972). The Portage Project: A model for early childhood education. *Exceptional Children, 38,* 210-217.

Shulman, L. (1998, February). *Teaching and teacher education among the professions.* The Hunt Lecture presented at the American Association of Colleges of Teacher Education Annual Meeting, New Orleans, LA.

Slavin, R. (1993). *The Study of Academic Instruction for Disadvantaged Students, Academic Challenge for the Children of Poverty* (Vol. 1, p. 359). Menlo Park, CA: SRI International.

Smith, M. L., & Glass, G. V. (1980). Meta-analysis of research on class size and its relationship to attitudes and instruction. *American Educational Research Journal, 17*(4), 419-423.

Stahl, B. J., & Lorenz, G. (1995). *Views on paraprofessionals.* St. Paul: Minnesota Department of Education.

Stringfield, S. (1999). *The impact on learner achievement of appropriately prepared and effectively integrated paraprofessionals.* Paper presented at the 18th annual conference of the National Resource Center for Paraprofessionals, Little Rock, AR.

Turney, D. T. (1962). *Secretaries for teachers.* Nashville, TN: Department of Education, George Peabody College for Teachers.

Udvari-Solnar, A. (1996). Examining teacher thinking: Constructing a process to design curricular adaptations. *Remedial and Special Education, 17*(4,) 245-254.

Index

CORWIN
PRESS

The Corwin Press logo—a raven striding across an open book—represents the happy union of courage and learning. We are a professional-level publisher of books and journals for K-12 educators, and we are committed to creating and providing resources that embody these qualities. Corwin's motto is "Success for All Learners."